FADING ADS OF

Birmingham

CHARLES BUCHANAN

PHOTOGRAPHY BY JONATHAN PURVIS

Charleston · London
THE
History
PRESS

Published by The History Press
Charleston, SC 29403
www.historypress.net

First published 2012

Manufactured in the United States

ISBN 978.1.60949.483.4

Library of Congress CIP data applied for.

For Carrie Beth.
Together we are stronger than white lead paint.

Contents

7   Foreword, by Tim Hollis

9   Acknowledgements

11   Author's Note

13   An Illustrated History

17   Advertising Ages

23   Walldog Days

29   Fading Out and Fading In?

33   Morris Avenue

45   Grocery Stores

51   Food

59   Retail

75   Industry

81   The Automotive District

89   Services

101   Entertainment

111   Places to Stay

117   Beverages

137   National Brands

155   Bibliography

167   About the Author

Foreword

Some of you may know that several years ago, one of my books was a volume titled *Vintage Birmingham Signs*. Keeping that in mind, realize that I am truly thankful that Charles Buchanan undertook the book you are now holding instead of me!

For reasons that Charles will explain as he goes along, trying to document any sort of history of Birmingham's fading brick wall signs presents challenges that I did not have when doing my own book, which was primarily concerned with neon signs. In fact, the challenges Charles had to overcome were a large part of why that book contained so few painted wall signs. Unlike the neon sign companies, whose owners—or at least their surviving family members—are still around, most of the companies that created the painted signs with which this book is concerned have vanished without a trace. That means their photo archives and other historical data have disappeared along with them—or at least are still hiding in some attic or basement, awaiting rediscovery.

So, armed with a camera, a notebook and precious little else, Charles has done a terrific job of documenting the stories behind the signs that still exist, some in better shape than others.

Of course, in vintage photos, there is a mother lode of painted signage that is long gone, either painted over or its surface demolished in the name of progress. That is not the focus of this book. Instead, Charles takes us on a journey through the painted signs that are sometimes "hidden in plain sight" and sometimes tucked away in the most obscure places. I can honestly say that while many of the signs discussed in this book are familiar to me, there are many others that I have never seen personally, even though I have repeatedly looked at the areas where they exist. Maybe it's time I got a new pair of glasses!

I have written many times about how my family spent a lot of time shopping in downtown Birmingham (at least when we weren't shopping at the huge G★E★S discount store on Lomb Avenue). Oddly, my own personal memories of Birmingham's signage run more toward the neon signs and billboards, but there were some of the painted type that became landmarks to me. One of these was the enormous PIZITZ lettering, in bold yellow and black, that adorned both the west and south sides of that magnificent store. Charles and I have discussed how, when the Pizitz family sold their business to McRae's in late 1986, the new owners must have had a steely-eyed determination to obliterate all traces of those two signs, because it appears that several layers of paint were used to blot them out. Amazingly, in recent years, the original letters (as well as a smaller rectangle reminding everyone that it was "Alabama's Largest Store") have begun to emerge from their cover-up job. Such is the power of the original paint that, if it still exists, one need only to wait and it will reappear sooner or later.

Perhaps the most spectacular example of this phenomenon is the giant wall on First Avenue North, described in detail by Charles, that features more "ghost signs" than you would find even in Casper's neighborhood. With Bull Durham and Nabisco competing for space, among others, it is obvious that the painters of each new sign would have done whatever possible to cover up the one underneath. After decades, pieces of them all have emerged, resulting in a huge version of one of those puzzles one is supposed to stare at until a clear picture appears.

Lest we think that all painted signs date back to grandpa's day, however, Charles also makes it clear that this is not a lost art. Some of the signage he documents was created as recently as the 1970s or 1980s, and there are still Birmingham companies willing to create new ones, should the need arise. When Morris Avenue was developed into an entertainment district in the 1970s, painted wall signs were used to try to recapture the desired gaslight-era flavor. The ironic part is that most of those 1970s signs are now gone, whereas examples dating back to the avenue's original heyday in the 1880s are still perfectly visible.

At this point, you are probably ready to get past this foreword and get on with the goodies contained in the rest of the book. (Well, why haven't you already turned the page, then?) I will shut up for now and let Charles do the talking from this point on, but since he consulted me for quotes and information, don't be surprised when I pop up again here and there. So, I will sign off by saying, "I'll see you all a little later!"

—Tim Hollis
birminghamrewound.com

Acknowledgements

When I began writing this book, I didn't know how much information I would be able to find on each ad. Details about the signs themselves—and the people and companies that painted them—are pretty scarce, and it took months of roundabout research to find the nuggets of Birmingham history hidden within the paint.

It was not a task that I could have done alone. Everyone listed below played a key role in helping me to tell the stories behind the signs, either by providing information and images or simply by pointing me in the right direction.

I especially want to thank Jonathan Purvis for his photography, which will help preserve the ads—in print, at least. And I also want to thank Doug Watts for our entertaining chats about sign painting and for his fifty years of hard work in the field. I hope that this book encourages a greater appreciation of the art and skill that he, Larry Rocks and other sign painters displayed on walls across the Birmingham area.

Graham Boettcher
Marc Bondarenko and Helene
 Taylor
Glenny Brock
Carrie Beth Buchanan
David Carrigan
Walt and Chatham Creel
Jeremy Erdreich
Steve Gilmer
Bill Gunn
Tim Hollis
Kevin Irwin
Jimmy and Sue Johnson

Deirdre Lewis
Jim Little
Will McKay
Cheryl Morgan
John Morse
Richard Neely
Amy Pate
David Pelfrey
Tim Pennycuff at the
 University of Alabama at
 Birmingham Archives
Jonathan Purvis
Larry Rocks

John and Tavis Sloan
Jennifer Taylor and Elizabeth
 Wells at Samford University
 Library Special Collection
Karen Utz at Sloss Furnaces
 National Historic Landmark
Don Veasey and Jim Baggett
 at the Birmingham Public
 Library Department of
 Archives and Manuscripts
Doug Watts
Carla Jean Whitley
Matt Windsor

Author's Note

This book spotlights a good portion of the fading ads on the walls of the Birmingham region, including signs that are familiar and a few that you have passed by every day without noticing. But there are many, many more out there. I'm still discovering them myself.

The total number of fading ads never remains constant. Every year, a few ads emerge from their slumber beneath coats of paint and panels of siding. At the same time, other ads vanish, worn into illegibility by sun and weather, concealed during a building renovation or obliterated in a demolition. This means that if you search for the ads in this book in person, there's a chance that you might not find them exactly as they appear here. (At least one has already disappeared under a new paint job.)

You're also going to see a lot of broken windows in these pages, which is not representative of the way all of metropolitan Birmingham looks. Fading ads often stick around the longest on buildings and in neighborhoods that have seen better days. But on the whole, Birmingham is a beautiful, green, vibrant city, and plenty of people are working hard to bring new energy to the areas in need of a spark.

Finally, I hope that this book will inspire you to explore Birmingham and learn more about the city around you. Use it as a guide to find the fading ads I've included and then start scouting for others. There's no telling what you'll discover if you look closely enough.

An Illustrated History

The past is easy to find in Birmingham. Just follow the signs.

They'll tell you which tobacco was "the standard of the world" and spotlight the soft drink that helped you "get wise." They'll direct you to the retailer that could sell you a horse-drawn wagon in 1886 and the building where you could store a piano in the 1920s. Who was a good mechanic for a Model T? What mill supplied the best chicken feed? The signs point the way. They can even recommend a century-old cure for indigestion—chewing gum, of course.

These fading advertisements, painted on the walls of the city and its suburbs, provide a pictorial history of the Birmingham area. They illuminate the everyday lives of the men and women who built an industrial boomtown in the heart of Alabama, revealing what they bought and where they shopped, stayed and played. While old photographs often give us an impression of the past as a black-and-white or sepia-toned world, the signs remind us that Birmingham's streets were alive with color. Wall after wall popped with bold text and crisp, detailed images glowing in bright whites, deep blacks and vivid reds, oranges, yellows, blues and greens. Every ad offered a picture of perfection—a cleaner wash, a fluffier cake, a better life with every purchase. They showcased the yearnings of a young, ambitious city.

GHOST STORIES

Today these ads are known as "ghost signs" because many pitch products and places that vanished long ago. But their current condition has something to do with it as well. Some ads have faded into mere wisps of words and shadows of color. A few are so transparent that they seem to materialize only when the morning or evening light is just right or in the thick, humid air following a rainstorm. The appearance—and ultimate disappearance—of a ghost sign depends on two factors: paint and weather.

While the ads were never designed to be permanent, they stick around because the paint used to create them contained lead carbonate. Sign painters mixed this "white lead" base with pigments, available as powder or mixed with linseed oil, to create colors, and the resulting thick, durable paints helped to preserve the walls.

Painted ads blanket the back wall of Loveman, Joseph and Loeb on Third Avenue North in the early twentieth century. This photo offers a good look at the size and detail of Birmingham's wall ads at the time, as well as how numerous they were. (Eagle-eyed viewers will spot at least two more painted walls in the distance. The billboards to the right of the mural likely were painted as well.) Loveman's became a leading department store after opening in Birmingham in 1887 and constructing "the largest store south of the Ohio" two years later. The giant ads would have disappeared in about 1916, when Loveman's built an annex next to the wall. Fire ultimately destroyed the wall and the rest of the main building in 1934. The Art Deco replacement now houses the McWane Science Center. The Alabama Theatre occupies the spot in the foreground where the two billboards sit. *Birmingham Rewound Collection.*

The painted ads "actually soaked *into* the brick," said Gus Holthaus, a Cincinnati sign painter quoted in William Stage's book *Ghost Signs: Brick Wall Signs in America.* "The paint they make today just lies on top of the brick."

The lead paints could withstand a lot of weather conditions, but summer's heat and winter's cold can take their toll on a wall, causing the bricks and paint to flake through expansion and contraction. Rain also contributes some wear and tear. However, Alabama's bright sunlight is perhaps the biggest culprit. The sun's ultraviolet radiation breaks down the chemical bonds in paint pigments, causing colors to fade. As a result, painted ads exposed to direct sunlight over the years are less sharp and legible than others protected by trees or neighboring buildings.

Some ads were completely sealed off from the elements, preserving the color and vibrancy of their youth. Often these signs were on exterior walls that became interior walls when a new building was constructed, or they disappeared behind concrete, plaster, stucco, siding or another coat of paint in a remodeling. In the past few decades, several frozen-in-time ads have reemerged as new businesses and residents fix up old buildings in downtown Birmingham. It's likely that many more of these treasures are buried in the walls, awaiting their own rediscovery.

Art or History?

"At the present time, I think that ads like these are considered by most to be historical items rather than works of art, but who knows how that might change? Early American trade signs and advertising figures can be found in the folk art collections of many major American museums. While advertisements painted on buildings aren't portable like early 19th-century trade signs, and therefore can't be brought into museums, perhaps in 100 years we'll revere them as examples of public mural art."

—Graham C. Boettcher, PhD, William Cary Hulsey Curator of American Art, Birmingham Museum of Art

DECIPHERING THE SIGNS

Birmingham did not experience as much of the urban renewal that transformed cities such as Atlanta and Charlotte in the last half of the twentieth century. Blocks of historic buildings still stand in the city center, as well as in the older suburbs. As a result, the Birmingham area is a veritable gallery of vintage painted ads.

But that doesn't make it any easier to figure out the stories behind the signs. True to their name, ghost signs present many mysteries. The messages that were once so clear to consumers can be confusing today.

Reading the ads often provides the first challenge. The degree of fading can make the text illegible, along with the fact that advertisers had no problem with painting over existing signs. Many would freshen up their displays each year by repainting ads in the same spot. Others would move into prime locations as soon as the previous leases expired, covering any existing ads with new ones for new products. As a result, the most popular walls are coated in layers of ads, and depending on how the paint has weathered, multiple ghosts can appear all jumbled together. Deciphering a sign sometimes requires a good deal of staring—and when that fails, fiddling with colors and contrast on a digital photo manipulation program can help.

Researching the history behind the signs calls for an indirect approach. Most of Birmingham's sign-painting companies have closed or merged into larger firms, and few records of their work exist today. Fortunately, information about the products and retailers promoted in the ads is more plentiful, along with the backstories of the buildings that host the signs. Old photographs also help to date the ads, though it's rare to see a painted sign as the subject of a photo. Most often, they appear in the backgrounds or off to the side. At the time, the painted walls were simply part of the landscape, much like billboards are for current consumers. Few people considered them historical artifacts.

But artifacts they have become, and their ghost stories are worth telling. These fading ads serve as reminders that we can let go of the past, but sometimes the past can't let go of us.

Advertising Ages

Many of the ghost signs still visible in American cities and small towns were created in the last century, but painted messages are nothing new; they date all the way back to Stone Age cave paintings.

Ancient cultures eagerly adapted the medium of painted walls for advertising. In the Roman city of Pompeii, for example, shopkeepers enticed customers with depictions of merchandise, brothels suggestively illustrated the available services and politicians promoted themselves along the main streets. Examples of each survived the eruption of Mount Vesuvius in AD 79 and excavation after 1,700 years buried in ash, making them perhaps the world's oldest ghost signs.

Businesses in Renaissance Europe kept painters busy creating both wall signs and wooden signs that hung from their buildings. Symbols of the goods and services for sale—such as a mortar and pestle to represent apothecaries and three gold balls to indicate a pawn broker—helped sell to a population that was largely illiterate. By the eighteenth century, some of the hanging signs had gotten so big that they were knocking people off their horses, prompting British authorities to pass laws requiring hypercompetitive shopkeepers to use only signs that were painted or mounted on walls.

American signage followed the European tradition, and by the end of the nineteenth century, some multistory buildings in large cities such as New York were covered top to bottom in painted text. These signs often listed the retailer's name and an exhaustive inventory of its offerings, much like a department store directory. The paint also kept pace with the country's westward expansion. Soon after the Civil War, it seemed that every fence, barn, bridge and abandoned building along America's highways and railroads was coated in advertising for patent medicine, tobacco, clothing, horse feed, local emporiums and much more. Wagons and boats became literal promotional vehicles. Even nature provided a canvas for enterprising sign makers. Visitors to Niagara gaped at the magnificent falls in addition to a huge ad for St. Jacob's Oil painted on an adjacent rock. Another patent medicine, S. T. 1860 X, illustrated cliffs and seemingly inaccessible rocks throughout the countryside.

In contrast, signage in the young city of Birmingham, founded in 1871 where key railroads crossed a region of untapped mineral

Dating from 1875, this photo by A.C. Oxford is perhaps the earliest to show a painted wall sign in Birmingham. Back then, the ads provided simple identification for buildings in the new town. The Linn Machine Shop was part of the Birmingham Foundry and Car Manufacturing Company, established by a Swedish sea captain turned banker named Charles Linn—the namesake of Linn Park. Located at the corner of First Avenue North and Fourteenth Street, it was one of the city's first foundries. *Samford University Library, Digital #D-000124.*

resources, was rather simple. The signs in an 1875 photograph of a foundry and machine shop—perhaps the earliest photo of a painted ad in Birmingham—do nothing more than identify the buildings. Other photos dating from the mid-1880s show ads beginning to pop up on brick walls. One sign promotes a "Horse Hotel" (a livery stable), while another declares Blackwell's Smoking Tobacco to be the "Best in the World." (Ads for this tobacco, also known as Bull Durham, got much bigger and bolder, as we will see in the final chapter.)

As the city's population grew, merchants and other businessmen painted their names near the rooflines of their buildings, and local and national advertisers staked their claims to blank brick walls, supplementing text with detailed illustrations of their products. Shifts in the predominant modes of transportation, from foot and horse-drawn carriage to streetcars and automobiles, forced ads to become bigger and more reliant on visuals over words. "Speed alters scale," wrote Michael J. Auer in a National Park Service brief on the preservation of historic signage. "The faster people travel, the bigger a sign has to be before they can see it." Well-traveled routes evolved into colorful avenues of painted advertising.

BIRMINGHAM SIGN SHOPS

The wall ads provided a lot of impact for a low price. And the money flowing in from clients fueled a local sign-painting industry that grew along with the city.

One of the earliest Birmingham directories, from 1883–84, lists two companies under "House and Sign Painters." George W. Harris was a "manufacturer of ready-mixed paints" who sold white leads, zinc whites, dry colors, colors in oil and Japan colors (concentrated paints sold as a paste). The other company, Narramore and Harry, also hung wallpaper. As advertising proliferated, so did the sign-painting businesses. In 1900, there were six; by 1930, the number had doubled.

The number of businesses listed as "sign painters and manufacturers" topped out at twenty-eight in 1958 and again in 1962. These listings included companies that specialized only in neon or other forms of advertising, but many sign shops handled everything. Dixie Neon, for

example, created painted signs with neon overlays that extended the ads' visibility after dark. Southern Ad Company told customers in 1916 to "See Us for Any Kind of Signs" and reported that it was the South's largest commercial sign shop, with the ability to create electric signs, as well as bulletins and wall ads. In 1953, the Modern Sign Company noted that it could handle real estate signs, repaints of neon signs, gold leaf, walls, truck lettering, silkscreen signs, office door lettering, show cards and highway reflecting signs. McBride Sign Company, which was founded in 1940 and eventually served national clients, touted walls along with "floats, street decorations, and complete holiday service—everything for a parade."

Plenty of smaller shops focused only on paint, however. The Two Vests sign shop, opened in 1886 by T. Frank Vest and his brother J.W. Vest, "do a general business of painting in every sort of sign work, a specialty of the house being fresco painting" (outdoor painting), notes an 1888 guide to Alabama cities. The book also calls them "thorough and conscientious artists," with a "very extensive trade all over this portion of the country." Other sign painters running their own shops included Alf Moore, Ned Green, Wallace Gammon and Henry Uhl.

African American sign painters or sign shops did not appear in the city directories of the late nineteenth and early twentieth centuries—many of which labeled black households and enterprises with a "(c)" or asterisk—despite the presence of thriving black-owned businesses that might have used their services. That does not mean that African American sign painters didn't exist in Birmingham; instead, they likely worked for white-owned sign shops.

AD PLACEMENT

America would have far fewer ghost signs today if not for the privilege system. It was a simple exchange that allowed advertisers to splash their signs on more walls—and big companies and small businesses both reaped the rewards.

Here's how it worked. An advertiser would strike a deal with a merchant to use the merchant's wall as the location for an ad. In return, the merchant would be promoted alongside the ad and get a freshly painted wall—and possibly some other goodies as well, including free product or perhaps new drapes. Soft drink advertisers especially latched on to this method and used it to build national campaigns. Most fading Coca-Cola wall ads, for example, were once privileges for local businesses.

The advertisers carefully selected the locations for their signs. A list of instructions from the Coca-Cola company reprinted in *Ghost Signs: Brick Wall Signs in America* explains that a wall isn't worth the trouble if it is obscured by trees, too small, too dilapidated or broken up by windows and doors or if it borders a narrow street. The company also nixed wall space that was too high. Though an ad several stories up could be seen far away, "People will not get cricks in their necks for Coca-Cola's benefit," the instructions note.

Obviously, advertisers liked placing privileges with merchants who sold their products, but they also coveted any highly visible wall in areas with heavy traffic. Leasing agents from

sign companies or the advertisers themselves would seek out property owners and offer money or other incentives—a gold watch perhaps—to secure the space. Sometimes these leasing agents were also the sign painters, which meant that the advertiser wasted no time in coating the wall with its message. This is how Clark Byers managed to cover more than nine hundred barns from Michigan to Florida with black-and-white ads for Rock City Gardens in Chattanooga, Tennessee. Willing farmers got a new paint job every two years, plus Rock City bathmats, thermometers and other knickknacks. Those wanting money got anywhere from three dollars to twenty.

A sign at 304 Twentieth Street South in Irondale offers a classic example of a privilege. In exchange for allowing Tip-Top Flour to paint its wall, the J.T. Ramsey and Son general merchandise store gained a mention in the ad. Mills around the country—including one in Birmingham, according to the fading words in the sign—produced the "mighty good" Tip-Top Flour. The ad may have been painted in the 1930s. *Author's photo.*

Walldog Days

Sign painters may be the most well-known unknown artists in history. Their work has been seen by millions of people and helped to earn billions of dollars, but it's rare to see a painted ad that bears their signatures.

That was no oversight or snub. Nearly all sign painters in the heyday of wall murals had artistic talent—which is evident in the meticulous attention to detail and clean brushwork—but they viewed their creations as more of a job to complete than as a piece of fine art. They knew that their ads might be painted over within a year. The fact that many of their signs have endured for decades is a happy accident.

So who were these pragmatic artists also known as "walldogs"? They were almost exclusively men, and they fell into two camps: the traveling sign painter and his urban cousin. Itinerant painters journeyed on rural routes and either picked up jobs in the small towns they visited or worked for advertising companies or clients, creating an entire campaign with every stop.

Urban sign painters, on the other hand, tended to cluster in sign shops, which were either independent or run by advertising companies. The menu of services in these shops often included far more than wall murals; painters also turned out show cards (ads painted on cards or paper), created wood and metal signs and added lettering and designs to glass windows and automobiles. These men were fearless, working atop a scaffold or on a small platform known as a stage that was suspended by ropes from the tops of tall buildings.

No matter where the sign painter worked, it was a dirty job—and a drinking job. Perhaps painting outdoors all day made them thirsty, or maybe they needed something to do while the paint dried, but the men with the brushes liked their liquor, and it became a stereotype that stuck to the industry.

WATCH AND LEARN

Doug Watts of Bessemer almost skipped becoming a sign painter because of their predilection for alcohol. "I think the paint fumes had something to do with their drinking," he said. "I was the only one who didn't drink." But Watts had been drawing since the age of seven

Photographs of sign painters at work in Birmingham are rare, if they exist at all, but this image of a crew in Ames, Iowa, taken by John Vachon in 1940, shows how the job has been done for more than a century. Initially, they outlined the letters and then filled them in—the task for the man kneeling on the ground. Then his partner, suspended from the ladders on a stage, "cuts in" around the letters and paints in the background. Finally, they will tackle the illustrated dog and moon on the left, adding detail and color to lines drawn with charcoal or a pounce bag full of chalk. Modern sign painters continue to use a similar process. *Library of Congress, Prints & Photographs Division, FSA/OWI Collection, LC-USF33-T01-001757-M2.*

and wanted a career where he could use his artistic talent.

At fifteen, he began working with Art Scott, a Bessemer sign painter "of the old school," for $2.50 a week for the first year. "In the old days, you had to serve a nine-year apprenticeship," Watts said. "It's actually one of the hardest trades to learn, and many sign painters were very secretive about their methods. You had to learn by watching." In some apprenticeships, the aspiring painter didn't get to touch an ad for years. "I learned how to clean brushes and cut out signs and things like that," added Watts. At night, he practiced drawing and painting letters of the alphabet. In time, he learned to paint walls, windows, displays, paper banners, show cards and designs on automobiles.

Larry Rocks, a professional sign designer who painted ads locally as well as in Chicago, said that the profession "was like a brotherhood. You had to know someone on the inside." He learned the trade in his father's Birmingham sign shop, which opened in 1938. "I started with walls, and as time went on, I learned to paint little letters and the gold leaf that we put on doors," he said.

letter was uniform and that enough space cushioned each element in the ad so that the images didn't bump into the words and vice versa. Other factors included the lettering style—block letters stand out more, but they require more precision than fancier scripts, Watts noted—and borders, which help contain the viewer's wandering eyes. Limited text also made the ads readable from a block—or five

FROM SKETCH TO WALL

Pushing a brush was just part of the sign painter's job. Developing the layout was the first step—and among the most important, said Watts, who worked for sign shops and then himself after his apprenticeship and military service in Vietnam. A good layout ensured that the width, height and thickness of each

With their legendary love of liquor, the painters assigned to this saloon probably enjoyed creating these ads. Many wall ads relied on intricate, colorful images not only to draw attention but also to spotlight specific products and packages. Sign painters were expected to be good illustrators, even with the help of grids and patterns. These liquor ads were painted in about 1913, when E.M. Perkinson's saloon opened on the corner of Second Avenue North and Twenty-third Street. The structure rising in the distance is the City Federal Building. *Birmingham, Alabama, Public Library Archives, file #1556.10.63.*

blocks—down the street. "The more letters, the more expensive the ads got," Watts said, adding, "There is truth in simplicity."

The sign painter would make a small sketch of the ad on paper, often using the client's words and images and adding specific measurements for each letter and element to ensure that everything would fit on the selected wall. Then it was time to go outside. Naturally, the challenge of using brick as a canvas is that it is rough and bumpy, and the ad's letters and pictures needed to be straight and even. Some sign painters smoothed out the rough spots by placing a grid over their drawing. Then, on the wall, they snapped chalk lines to create a larger grid. The two grids enabled the painters to draw the ad to scale—with one inch on paper translating to one foot on the wall—using a piece of charcoal to create a rough outline.

Another technique dates to the days of Renaissance painters. Sign painters would draw the ad's design on paper and then run over the lines with a perforating wheel, similar to a sewing tool. At the wall, they would place the paper pattern against the wall and "pounce" over the tiny holes with a cloth bag full of chalk, which would transfer a dotted outline of the design onto the brick. Rocks said that in Chicago, the big sign shops would use projectors to enlarge the drawings and then mechanically punch them. All of that would happen at night, and trucks full of patterns would be waiting for the sign painters each morning.

Patterns and pounce wheels allowed the sign makers to create the same ads on different walls, which was crucial for many promotional campaigns. "The ability to duplicate a sign was one of the marks of a good sign painter," Watts emphasized.

Even with assistance from grids and patterns, sign painters had to take special care with drawing letters. The best technique was to start in the center and work out to the sides, said both Rocks and Watts. "If you start on one end, you'll discover that your margin won't be right when you get to the other end," Rocks added. Walls are more forgiving than other forms of signage, Watts noted, adding that letters on walls can be fudged by a few inches to fix spacing that is a little awry. Many a sign maker also relied on the horizontal lines of mortar between rows of bricks to serve as guides to keep letters running in straight lines and counted bricks to ensure that letter width was uniform.

COLOR SMART

Until the 1930s, sign painters had to create their own paints, mixing the white lead with the pigments in a process that could take at least an hour. In his *Ghost Signs* book, William Stage noted that these paints produced flatter finishes than current paints, but they could handle weather better as well. The colors were pure and vibrant, with evocative names such as lampblack, yellow chrome, Naples yellow, yellow ochre, sienna, Indian red, vermilion, scarlet lake, rose madder, ivory drop black, Prussian blue, ultramarine blue and emerald green.

Watts faced a particular challenge when it came to selecting paint: he is colorblind. "But I'm not color stupid," he said. "I know what color combinations make up other colors." Indeed, sign painters have been compared to alchemists, devising their own formulas to create different shades.

Of course, many sign painters ended up with lead poisoning from years of exposure to the paint. Some of its symptoms, such as mental and physical sluggishness and heightened irritability, may have been mistaken for drunkenness, contributing to the stereotype of sign painters as alcoholics.

In the late 1970s, federal law banned lead from nearly all paints produced and sold in the United States, and sign painters had to look for new options. Rocks said that latex paints allow walls to "breathe" better, but Watts prefers enamel paints because they contain more pigment than latex.

BRUSHES AND SANDBAGS

The brush of choice was called a fitch, made of pig's hair with an angled edge. Rocks said that these gave the best detail, and painters preferred them for creating outlines of letters and visuals on the rough walls. "We altered the pressure on the brush every time we came to a bump," he said.

Brushes weren't the only tools of the trade. A maulstick is "a little stick with a ball on the end of it that some artists use to prop the hand holding the brush," Watts explained. "It can assist you really well in painting a sign." Many painters also carried one of the many available sign-painting handbooks, which offered advice on color mixing, surface preparation and lettering rules, among other topics. *The Expert*

Sign Painter, written by A. Ashmun Kelly in 1911, dispensed helpful wisdom such as: "A tinge of blue in white lettering color on a black ground will increase its strength" and "A badly colored sign will look vile, no matter how well the lettering is done." More sage advice: "Never do a brick wall sign in cold or wet weather, if it can be avoided. Dampness will cause the paint to perish."

In practice, however, sign painters often worked in all kinds of conditions, from blazing heat to bone-chilling cold—extremes that became magnified on a swinging piece of metal or wood several stories high against the side of a brick wall. The precarious nature of their workspace didn't faze many painters, however. "I did a three-story-high wall for a department store in downtown Birmingham, and all we had were four-by-four posts that we hung off the top of the building," recalled Watts, who worked for Central Sign and Advertising Company at the time. "We put sandbags on one end of the four-by-fours and hung the stage off the other end."

Watts ended up painting that ad by himself, but most sign painters worked in teams of two. "The crews had a journeyman and a helper," Rocks said. "They basically did the same thing, but the journeyman was in charge, and in Chicago, there was only one dollar's difference in hourly pay. Sometimes a guy would work as a helper for fifteen years."

Painters were expected to complete ads quickly, no matter how many people handled the job. When Rocks worked in Chicago, his crew often had to wait until 9:00 a.m. to get started because the mornings were so cold, but they could finish large signs—even ones twelve feet tall by forty feet wide—by midafternoon.

"There was no wasted motion," he said. Watts noted that years of experience helped him work fast. He painted the three-story department store ad in one day.

TRICKS OF THE TRADE

Of course, the longtime painters learned a few tricks to make their jobs easier. To save time and paint, Rocks's crews didn't put background color under big letters. "We took a felt-tip pen and made a dot pattern around the letters," he said. "Then we added the finish coat to the background everywhere else. Where you brushed over the line, the pen would bleed through. Then you could come back and paint the inside of the letters."

Watts relied on a few visual techniques to ensure that his ads looked good from fifty or more feet away. "Round letters like O and S are the hardest to paint," he said. To keep them even with other text, "the tops and bottoms of those letters have to go above and below your guide lines. When you back away, those letters will shrink to line up with the others because the eyeball is not perfectly round. You have to fool the eye." The thickness of round letters also varies because "there's nowhere for the eye to stop, unlike the square sides on other letters." Many sign makers used contrasting colors and painted highlights and shadows to increase the visibility of their ads.

WALLDOGS TODAY

Even though painted wall ads have been supplanted as the major outdoor advertising medium by billboards and vinyl signs, you can still see sign painters at work. In large urban areas like New York, national advertisers turn to walldogs to create ads on the sides of buildings, though not in the quantity of a century ago. And new ads are in demand in smaller cities such as Birmingham, where some businesses choose the handcrafted, historic feel of painted signs over plastic or vinyl versions. (More on that in the next chapter.)

Books and at least one documentary film, *The Sign Painter Movie*, also have sparked interest in the art and work of the American walldog. It's a refreshing change for the previous generation, including Watts, now retired after fifty years on the job. "There's not very much creativity in signs anymore because a machine does it," said Watts, who still dips his brushes in motor oil or petroleum jelly to keep them clean. "I used to be able to tell who painted what just by looking at it. Those old signs had character."

Fading Out and Fading In?

Painted walls, once the dominant form of outdoor advertising, began to decline once advertisers saw the light—of electrical and neon signs. The illuminated ads, which first appeared in the United States in the early twentieth century, offered an exciting alternative to the static walls, with the added bonus of being readable twenty-four hours a day.

But the billboard struck the bigger blow. When billboard companies adopted national size standards in 1900, advertisers began incorporating them into national campaigns. They also appealed to the bottom line: the boards were cheaper to construct and maintain than painted ads and required far less labor, and while painted billboards did exist, most featured printed paper that could be switched out quickly and often. Billboards also could fit into urban locations that wouldn't work for wall ads and could follow automobiles out of the cities and down the highways.

Today, the slick ads on most billboards are printed on vinyl, a durable alternative to paper. "With vinyl I can produce so much more," said Larry Rocks, the former painter in Birmingham who now designs signs on vinyl. "I wouldn't

use paint on my own sign unless I wanted an antique look."

Changes to the urban environment in Birmingham, as in other American cities, contributed to the decline of painted ads in favor of billboards. The rise of suburban communities and the construction of highways took jobs and residents out of the central city, away from the tall brick walls. At the same time, downtown urban renewal projects and the demolition of many older structures for parking lots also completely removed some of the available wall space.

REACHING THE LIMITS

The few new painted wall signs that appeared in Birmingham in the 1970s and 1980s faced another challenge that their predecessors had not: sign regulation.

The glut of advertising signage that literally covered some cities in the early decades of the twentieth century finally irritated enough people that governments added signage regulations to their zoning ordinances. The

United States Supreme Court upheld such laws in the 1954 *Berman v. Parker* ruling, saying that "[i]t is within the power of the legislature to determine that the community should be beautiful as well as healthy, spacious as well as clean, well balanced as well as carefully patrolled."

The old painted ads, along with some neon signs, got a bad rap in the decades after that ruling. In many cities, the overwhelming opinion considered them junky and outdated—a blight on the cityscape. *Birmingham* magazine's 1971 issue marking the city's centennial looked forward to laws that would "transform visual pollution into a clean, spacious environment. Additional ordinances could require the remodeling or removal of signs from abandoned buildings." (The same article also called for a network of skybridges downtown.)

The zoning ordinance that did come about in Birmingham, like those in many other cities, regulates the size, number and location of signs. For example, building wall signs cannot exceed 15 percent of the wall, up to a maximum size of 150 square feet, though an exception allows up to 210 square feet depending on how far back the building is from its property line. The city's code does not include any specifications about historic painted ads.

REVIEW AND REVIVAL

The city's Design Review Committee enforces additional rules that apply to Birmingham's eight historic districts and twenty-seven commercial revitalization districts, set up to encourage reinvestment in specific areas of the city. Formed in 1979, the appointed group includes architects, landscape architects, builders and citizens "interested in the legacy and history of the city," said Cheryl Morgan, a committee member, architect and director of Auburn University's Birmingham-based Urban Studio. Together, they review plans for new buildings and renovations, along with requests for signage, checking them against the specific rules unique to each district. Their decisions affect everything from paint colors to lighting to landscaping. "The intention is to protect the integrity of each neighborhood and give people confidence that their investment is going to retain its value," Morgan said. "It's an important part of the toolbox for economic development."

Tastes and perspectives change depending on the makeup of the committee, Morgan noted, but "right now there's a lot of enthusiasm for a variety of good signs. It's very exciting to see some new murals happening." In fact, a mini revival of painted wall ads seems to be underway in Birmingham. Several businesses in the central city—including a restaurant, two breweries and a canine day care—are drawing attention with large, colorful new signs coating their façades. Jimmy Johnson, the owner of Dog Days of Birmingham, said that his ad, covering the entire side of his building, is worth its cost because it has brought in new customers—and even some people without dogs who want to know more about the business behind the mural.

A BRIGHT FUTURE

The topic of restoration always comes up when fading ads are in the picture, and for Richard and John Neely, it has become a hobby. The brothers restored the wall ads at Sloss Furnaces (see the chapter on Industry) along with two in Bessemer: a 1920s Coca-Cola privilege for the Sam Raine & Company Square-Deal Bakery and a 1904 sign promoting J. Colley's wholesale wines, whiskey and beers. Next on their list is an ad for a former buggy dealership.

Richard, who is a history professor, said that he and John share an enthusiasm for the past and that their love of signs was inspired by their grandfather's country store, which featured a big ad on its wall. "We drive around the city and wonder what it looked like when it was painted up with advertisements," Richard said. "Everywhere you looked was color. It was extremely bright."

Their efforts to recapture that color have encouraged people to talk about the history of the city and recall visits to long-gone businesses, Richard said. But they also have received some unusual questions. "When we restored the sign for whiskey and beers, we must have had more than twenty people ask us when we were opening," he recalled. "We told them they're about one hundred years too late."

Others have mixed feelings about the restoration of ghost signs, suggesting that the freshly painted ads look out of place when everyone is used to seeing them in a faded state. Birmingham historian Tim Hollis said, "It's great to keep them from fading away, but sometimes it just isn't the same. It's like someone painted a new sign where an old one used to be, and you aren't able to see the original anymore."

Whether faded or restored, painted wall ads in Birmingham seem to have reached a new audience that views them as an integral part of the cityscape—and the city's character. When a Sentinel TV ad faced the possibility of removal in 2012, the public reaction was swift and vocal, and the mural now will remain in place. (See the chapter on Entertainment for the story.)

In a National Park Service preservation brief about historic signs, Michael J. Auer provided a perfect description of the role these ads now play:

> Signs often become so important to a community that they are valued long after their role as commercial markers has ceased. They become landmarks, loved...for their familiarity, their beauty, their humor, their size, or even their grotesqueness...When signs reach this stage, they accumulate rich layers of meaning. They no longer merely advertise, but are valued in and of themselves. They become icons.

Birmingham architect Jeremy Erdreich put it even more succinctly in a blog post written about the threat to the Sentinel TV ad. These signs "make the public space we move through unique," he wrote. "Without them we have just a bunch of...brick walls."

Morris Avenue

With no major waterway running through Jones Valley, the railroads served as Birmingham's river, and Morris Avenue was its bustling port. Trains could pull up alongside warehouses that lined the street, accommodating the exchange of raw materials and manufactured goods between the city and the rest of the world.

Morris Avenue is located in the center of Birmingham, inside the "Railroad Reservation." In the original 1871 city plan, this land formed a buffer for the railroad tracks that roll through the heart of the community, and it was reserved for "mechanical enterprises" (such as factories) that required easy access to transportation. The prominent avenue, one of the few in the city plan with a name instead of a number, honors Josiah Morris, the financial advisor and largest stockholder for the Elyton Land Company, the real estate firm that founded Birmingham. Without his support, the concept of an industrial city in central Alabama would never have become reality.

Due to its prime location, Morris Avenue quickly grew into Birmingham's wholesale district. By the 1880s, sturdy brick warehouses "were built to house small family enterprises which sold fruits, groceries, spices, coffee, tea, meal, and flour, and ran sawmills, stockyards, and carriage works on the busy thoroughfare," wrote historian Marjorie White. Regional and national companies also established outposts, and other businesses, from printers to paint wholesalers, joined the mix. City directories from the early twentieth century include a roster of evocative names: the J. Caravella Fruit Company, the Schwartzchild and Sulzberger Beef Company, Antognoli and Allegri merchandise brokers, the Greek-American Produce Company, the Alabama Candy Company and the Kant Printing House, among others.

The cobblestone street was a hive of activity. In the 1980 Birmingfind study, Charlie LaRocca described visits to Morris Avenue with his father, an Italian fruit peddler who purchased produce and groceries there. Wagons backed up to each building, he said, and they were packed in so tightly that horses had to move their heads to let vehicles pass. "There was a café on the right named L&N Cafe; then there was a fish house—you could smell the fish; and on the left, you could smell chickens; and then there was the peanut house, and you could smell peanuts roasting," LaRocca recalled. "So, every step that you took on Morris Avenue, you could

Above: Morris Avenue teems with horse-drawn traffic in this westward view from Twenty-second Street. Beneath painted ads, the wagons pick up wholesale goods to deliver to stores and homes across Birmingham. This scene was captured between 1902, when the tall Woodward Building in the background was completed, and 1912, when the skyscraping John Hand Building would have blocked that view. Though Morris Avenue has changed over a century, one food wholesaler remains on the street. The Peanut Depot, founded in 1907, continues to sell bags of hot peanuts fresh from the roaster. *Birmingham, Alabama, Public Library Archives, file #1556.20.98.*

Opposite: Tyler's hunting dog looks sharp and fresh in this photo dating from the years after 1915, when the company moved into its Morris Avenue warehouse. A company print ad from 1924 notes, "We use a Pointer Dog as our trade-mark, and our motto, 'Tyler's Best: this dog stands for quality, we stand behind the dog,' means just that." *Birmingham, Alabama, Public Library Archives, file #OVH395.*

be blindfolded, but you knew what you were coming to next by the smell."

The worst smell, LaRocca said, emanated from the potato seller. With no refrigeration, "when the potatoes got hot, they'd go bad. I hated to go by that place because it was terrible."

By the 1970s, most of the wholesale firms had moved out, and the street, designated a National Historic District, was ripe for redevelopment. The "Old Town Uptown" project created an entertainment district of nightclubs, restaurants and performance spaces that filled the old warehouses. The city spruced up the avenue and hailed it as Birmingham's Bourbon Street. Unfortunately, a high-profile crime in 1977 wrecked Old Town's momentum, frightening away potential customers from a night out in the city.

The empty spaces left behind would pave the way for another comeback. Low rents, a prime downtown location and wide-open, easily adaptable interiors attracted architects, designers, attorneys, accountants, real estate specialists and residents. Renovating buildings into loft condominiums and commercial spaces added modern amenities while preserving the original brickwork, heart-pine floors, tall ceilings and large industrial windows with views of the city and railroad. Today, Morris Avenue is a quieter street—and a far less smelly one—than it was in its wholesale heyday, but it is alive again.

With Morris Avenue's history, it's no wonder that it boasts the greatest concentration of fading ads in Birmingham. In a wholesale district of the late nineteenth and early twentieth centuries, a seller's building was its biggest advertisement. A company's name, painted in large, bold letters high on the façade, helped potential buyers to navigate the crowded streets. Closer to the ground, detailed depictions of the products for sale provided further direction. Many of the advertisements on Morris Avenue have faded beyond recognition, but a few still offer a faint glimpse of the street's busiest era.

TYLER GROCERY COMPANY

In 1915, after surviving fires in two other locations in town, Tyler Grocery Company moved into a large warehouse that spans a block between the western end of Morris Avenue and First Avenue North. The

If you squint and stare at this ad for Tyler Grocery Company, you might see the last traces of the painted hunting dog that served as the wholesaler's trademark. A faded tag below the ad, which faces the 1600 block of Morris Avenue, attributes it to the Daniel Sign Company. *Jonathan Purvis.*

painted ad dominating one wall of the four-story building may date from that time. Unfortunately, only a shadow remains of the illustrated hunting dog that served as the ad's focal point, and the words "This Dog Stands for Quality" and "Tyler's Best" are about to bound off into history alongside it.

Tyler Grocery was a wholesaler of canned fruit, canned vegetables and coffee, with distribution centers in Tuscaloosa, Jasper and Fayette, Alabama, in addition to Birmingham. In about 1934, the company moved to Vanderbilt Road, close to a rail yard northeast of downtown Birmingham; it ceased operations just a year or two later.

Later, the Tyler Grocery building became a merchandise storage warehouse, first for Sears, Roebuck and Company and then, in the 1950s, for Pizitz, an iconic Birmingham-based department store chain. A merger removed the Pizitz name from retailing in 1987, but Pizitz signs still remain on the loading dock of the vacant old warehouse. Shielded from the sun by an overhang, the signs look freshly painted, as if they are awaiting the next delivery.

SOUTHERN SUPPLY AND EXTRACT/STANDARD DISINFECTANT/DIXIE CHEMICAL

The faded, smudged sign on the back wall of the building at 1625–1627 First Avenue North was once quite wordy, listing the goods for sale inside, but today only a few items remain clear. The "extracts" and "syrups" in the ad belonged either to the Marx-Rich Cider and Grocery Company, a soft drink manufacturer located at that address in 1909, or to the Southern Supply and Extract Company, which occupied the space by 1913.

The latter company produced syrups and extracts to add flavor and color to candy, ice cream and sodas, and it also manufactured a soft drink named Deacon Brown. According to Dennis Smith's history of Birmingham sodas, the Deacon Brown home office was in Montgomery, Alabama, and a bottling company—perhaps an outgrowth of the Marx-Rich firm—opened in this building in 1911. The next year, the Deacon Brown Manufacturing Company went bankrupt, and Southern Supply and Extract bought the drink's formula and trademark. Deacon Brown shipped from this building's back door until 1914, when

Birmingham's Nifty Syrup Company, producers of Nifty Cola, acquired the drink.

Standard Disinfectant Company arrived in 1914 after Southern Supply and Extract moved out. The firm, which manufactured oils and paints along with disinfectants, left its mark by painting its name across the top of the back wall. By 1919, Standard had become the Dixie Chemical Products Company, which was supplanted by the Dixie Asbestos Company in about 1925. The name "Dixie" is barely readable in the painted smudge above the door in the wall. Since then, tenants have included a variety of small businesses, from a paint seller to a hair salon.

A jumble of words reveals the early history of this building that backs up to the 1600 block of Morris Avenue. Two soft drink manufacturers produced the "extracts" and "syrups" (listed on either side of the door) between 1909 and 1914. Soon afterward, Standard Disinfectant Company and Dixie Chemical Products Company added their names to the wall. As newer coats of paint have faded, the three layers of white-lead letters have melded together. *Jonathan Purvis.*

The wall with the fading ads offers another clue to the building's past. Set at an unusual angle, it traces the path of a railroad spur that led to the back door for easy loading of bottles of Deacon Brown or disinfectant. When the two-story building was new, tracks blanketed the area behind it, forming a vast freight yard for the Louisville & Nashville Railroad, complete with a roundhouse for locomotives. A 1930s project to elevate the railroads through downtown Birmingham made the old rail yard obsolete, and today it is simply a grassy open space overlooked by whispers of painted words.

GOLBRO

Birmingham's rapid growth at the turn of the twentieth century attracted more than just factory workers from Alabama's small towns and rural counties. Entrepreneurs also flocked to the young city, opening retail establishments to meet every consumer need.

Sam Goldstein was among them. Already a success in the east-central Alabama town of Talladega, where he had started a small dry goods store in 1895, Goldstein opened a business in Birmingham in 1902 and brought his five sons into the company. Goldstein Brothers—eventually shortened to Golbro— was, at various times, a department store, a pawn shop and a showroom in which customers purchased memberships that enabled them to buy jewelry, housewares and sporting goods at discounted prices. Jim Little, who worked in the Golbro store behind the giant ad, said that the paid membership was dropped when similar competitors moved into the market.

Jewelry became the company's main focus. "Over time, we would build up our 'book' of customers," Little said. "We knew what our customers wanted, and for birthdays and

anniversaries, we always had jewelry picked out for them to purchase."

"All of the Goldstein family members worked in the stores—aunts, uncles, children and grandchildren," Little added. "They took care of their own family members and the family of employees that worked for them."

The Golbro ad went up after 1960, when the company opened its flagship store and corporate headquarters in the four-story building, a former hardware store built around the turn of the twentieth century. The main entrance opened onto First Avenue North. Downtown Birmingham was still a major shopping destination at the time, and the store benefited from its proximity to the city's biggest retailers.

By the 1970s, Golbro spanned the state, with ten stores in locations from Huntsville to Mobile. In addition to jewelry, the chain sold crystal, china, ceramics, brass pieces, clocks, luggage and children's furniture. From 1950 to 1990, the company also produced its own mail-order catalogue.

Declining sales prompted Golbro to shutter the First Avenue store in 1990. Five years later, the chain, by then the second-oldest jeweler in Birmingham, went bankrupt and closed after a century in business. In 2002, the Golbro building and the adjacent office building were remodeled into Jemison Flats, a development that includes lofts and office spaces. Part of the former jewelry showroom now houses a fitness center for residents.

A large ad for Golbro jewelers faces Terry Beckham's untitled art piece from the Birmingham Mural Project on the 1800 block of Morris Avenue. The Golbro ad appeared after 1960, and the unusual image of a tree followed in 1979 as part of an initiative to beautify walls around downtown and provide jobs to artists. *Jonathan Purvis.*

UNTITLED TREE MURAL

Not all ghost signs in Birmingham advertise a product or service. Some are designed to be works of art in themselves.

The untitled image of an uprooted tree that faces Morris Avenue at Nineteenth Street is one of thirteen murals by ten artists painted in 1978 and 1979 in a program to provide jobs for artists and to add color to blank, deteriorating walls around the city. The Birmingham Mural Project was sponsored by the Greater Birmingham Arts Alliance (GBAA) and supported by the federal Comprehensive Employment and Training Act, aimed at improving employment prospects and job skills among economically disadvantaged populations, including minorities, people with disabilities and those who have a hard time finding a job even when the economy is strong.

Each artist hired by the GBAA had to identify a highly visible location for a mural and gain permission from the property owner, who also had final approval over the design. Terry Beckham, who created the tree on Morris Avenue, offered a little direction. "I showed them two really bad drawings and the one I really wanted to do," he said in Laurie K. Long's essay "A City with a Face: Street Art in Birmingham." Artists also had to repair, clean, seal and prime their brick canvases—not an easy task on such a large scale.

Beckham chose the Stallings Building as the site for his mural. Constructed in 1909, it originally housed the city's chamber of commerce and offices of the Lincoln Reserve Life Insurance Company. For years, the back wall carried painted ads for Lincoln Life and messages promoting Birmingham. One proclaimed the city to be "The

World's Cheapest Center for Making Pig Iron and Steel."

Beckham's mural covers those old ads with more than five thousand square feet of paint. He completed the piece in July 1979 after three months of work, and it quickly became one of the project's most visible and well-known images. "It is centrally located and can be seen from many angles at a considerable distance," Long wrote. "It is a gigantic 'stamp' of nature set in an urban environment, and while not detracting from or clashing with that environment, it commands attention from passersby. The mural has become a veritable landmark in the downtown area, and…lends a distinct accent to the city's atmosphere."

Though the murals won support from the public and local businesses, federal funding for the project ended in September 1979. Today, Beckham's work is one of the few remaining pieces—many walls have been repainted, or buildings have been torn down or renovated. The 2002 conversion of the Stallings Building into the Jemison Flats condominiums punched several windows through the mural, but the mysterious tree continues to float above Morris Avenue, now providing an artistic backdrop to a pocket-sized green space.

under the management of his son, Walter Booth, in 1924. In addition to a large ad on the building's eastern side, the company painted smaller signs on western and front façades.

An ad for Nucoa margarine covered the original sign either before the Booth family left the space in the 1930s or after another grocery wholesaler moved in behind them. Nucoa, containing hardened coconut oil as its main ingredient, was hailed as a major advance in product quality upon its introduction in 1917; it became the country's top-selling brand of margarine for three decades.

Until 1950, margarine was actually restricted by federal law. The dairy lobby, in an attempt to protect butter sales, encouraged Congress to tax margarine at two cents per pound. It also convinced lawmakers in thirty states to ban yellow dyes in margarine, which is normally white, so that it wouldn't resemble butter. (Some states even required it to be dyed pink.) Most states repealed their laws in the 1950s and 1960s as the demand for margarine grew.

The Booth building, constructed in the last part of the nineteenth century, found an unusual use in the 1970s. The entire first floor was reconfigured as a drive-through teller for a bank located on First Avenue North. Customers would drive into the building from

T.M. BOOTH AND SON/ NUCOA

Thomas Booth was a wholesale grocer from Pulaski, Tennessee, who specialized in butter, eggs and poultry. He founded his company in 1887, and the Birmingham branch opened

According to an ad in a city directory, T.M. Booth and Son was one of Tennessee's oldest produce firms when it opened a branch at 2018 Morris Avenue in 1924. The later ad, for Nucoa margarine (visible above "poultry"), could have been painted before the Booths left the premises in the 1930s—if they sold the product—or another wholesaler who followed them might have added it in the 1940s. One of the signs, probably the Nucoa ad, is credited to "O'Connor." *Jonathan Purvis.*

Morris Avenue and exit through a First Avenue storefront. This "tunnel" was enclosed in the 1980s when the building became office space, which it still is today.

BURWELL, SLATON AND McGLATHERY

After 125 years, the painted words "Wagons, Buggies, Stages, Harnesses" hold the title of Birmingham's oldest visible ghost sign. In 1886, just 15 years after the city's founding, T.O. Burwell, S.W. Slaton and W.W. McGlathery built this warehouse for their two-year-old business,

which sold all kinds of equipment necessary for horse-drawn transportation, along with cotton, agricultural implements and fertilizer. The wide central doors that enabled the partners to move wagons and carriages in and out of the building also remain.

A year later, a Jefferson County guidebook hailed the entrepreneurial efforts of the three young men: "By their energy, perseverance, and commendable personal qualities, [they] have established the only reliable and profitable wagon trade in Birmingham." However, by 1889, the company was out of business, and its warehouse later was used for feed and grain sales and as a place to store farm machinery for the Yeilding department store. Burwell, Slaton and

Birmingham's oldest fading ad clings to the bricks of the former Burwell, Slaton and McGlathery warehouse, built at 2125 Morris Avenue in 1886. For three years, the company sold wagons, buggies, stages and harnesses here. A sign for a later tenant, a grain company, also holds on just under the roofline. *Jonathan Purvis.*

McGlathery's sign disappeared under coat after coat of paint.

During Morris Avenue's stint as an entertainment district, the building became Oaks Street, a collection of restaurants, shops and a theater. A large new painted sign identifying the business appeared on the side of the building, by then surrounded by parking lots instead of other warehouses. Oaks Street owner Randall Oaks helped to lead the movement to save Sloss Furnaces from demolition, and the first meetings of the group that became the Sloss Furnaces Association were held in the restaurant.

A law firm replaced Oaks Street in the early 1980s and launched a full renovation, which included the removal of the paint from the façade. It must have taken a lot of

hard work to peel away all the layers down to the brick, but the original one proved to be the toughest. Burwell, Slaton and McGlathery's ad had actually become part of the building, serving as a permanent reminder of Birmingham's early days.

ALAGA SYRUP

This sign is sure to trigger happy memories of waking up to a breakfast of warm biscuits topped with sweet syrup. Alaga is a sugar cane–flavored syrup that has been made by Whitfield Foods (formerly the Alabama-Georgia Syrup Company) of Montgomery since 1906.

Rural Alabamians once used cane and sorghum syrups as sweeteners instead of refined sugar, in part because they could grow the source crops and cook the syrups themselves. Communities often shared a mule-operated syrup mill or were visited by syrup makers each fall. In a 2007 *Birmingham News* article, Paul Mask, an official with the Alabama Cooperative Extension Service, recounted that the state once had "a north–south fault line. Syrup made from sugar cane dominated from Montgomery south, while sorghum syrup dominated in northern Alabama."

Though Birmingham was home to its own syrup company—Yellow Label Syrup—Alaga was popular in the city. Old photographs even show large illuminated signs advertising Alaga from atop downtown buildings. In 1939, Sam Spina, a wholesale grocery company that marketed Whitfield's products, moved into this Morris Avenue warehouse that had once stored flour, grain and bananas. The firm painted ads along its two façades—the Alaga sign got a prime position one story above ground level,

along the heavily traveled Twenty-second Street viaduct. In bright red, white and yellow, the ad declared Alaga to be "The Quality Syrup" and "Good Every Drop." Down on Morris Avenue, the second ad promoted something a little more sour: Whitfield's Alabam Girl pickles.

While the pickle ad is long gone, the Alaga sign made a colorful reappearance in 2010. It had been painted over by 1950, replaced with a plain ad for the Sam Spina company. By the late 1970s, the wall along the viaduct was the canvas

The Alaga syrup ad on the second story of 2201 Morris Avenue—facing the Twenty-second Street viaduct—has been around since about 1939, when a wholesale grocer who sold the product moved into the building. Many Birmingham natives know this wall as the site of *Geo-Chromatic Progress*, a striped mural that Michael Mojher painted in the late 1970s. The ad for "the Quality Syrup" that is "Good Every Drop" came back to light in 2010, when the mural and many other coats of paint were removed. Look closely to see letters from an older ad for a produce company behind the Alaga name. *Jonathan Purvis.*

for *Geo-Chromatic Progress*, a striking striped art piece created by Michael Mojher for the Birmingham Mural Project. The work became a landmark for many locals, including architect, historian and photographer John Morse, who first saw it as a child. "I appreciated its jazzy rhythms and palette at first sight," he said. "Over time it became one of my favorite scraps of the urban fabric" and a common subject of his photographs.

A beige coat of paint covered the fading mural in 2009, much to the chagrin of graffiti artists Daze, Roke and Priest, who embellished the blandness with a painting of a little girl pulling down the corner of the wall to reveal the mural. Finally, the building owners stripped away everything—the graffiti girl, the beige, the mural and the paint below them, revealing the Alaga sign peeking around a series of windows added during a renovation of the old warehouse.

While the former Spina building waits for a new tenant, Whitfield has secured its position as the state's largest commercial cane syrup producer. Alaga is sold throughout the South and in cities such as Chicago and Detroit, providing a sweet taste of home for southerners who moved to find jobs and freedom from discrimination in the twentieth century. It's also an ingredient in dozens of recipes, from hot wings to baked beans, and it is a popular item in the concession stand at Montgomery's baseball park, where fans can enjoy biscuits with Alaga syrup while watching a team named, appropriately, the Biscuits.

Grocery Stores

Long before the arrival of supermarkets, food stores understood the power of a prime location. Small markets followed the city's spread throughout Jones Valley, capturing highly visible lots on corners and along streetcar lines. In 1932, for example, the Birmingham area included more than 750 grocery stores operated by more than six hundred proprietors, placing fresh produce, meats and packaged goods within easy walking distance of most homes.

A majority of Birmingham's markets were of the mom and pop variety, operated by families in small spaces packed with merchandise. Often, the family lived above or behind the store, with each member working there in some capacity.

Many of those families also were immigrants—mainly Italians, Greeks and Lebanese who came to Birmingham to work industrial jobs but found more lucrative opportunities outside the mines and mills. The Birmingfind study of the early 1980s noted that groceries were popular ventures for immigrants because they didn't require a lot of monetary investment or much English to open the doors. Some found success by locating their markets in African American neighborhoods that didn't have stores. By the 1930s, Italians were operating more than three hundred local grocery stores, the study notes, and ownership had become a symbol of progress among the local Italian immigrant community. Earlier, in 1902, a Birmingham newspaper declared that Greek immigrants had a monopoly on the city's fruit stands. And at one point in time, the Southside neighborhood boasted more than twenty Lebanese-owned grocery stores.

The growth of supermarkets swept away most of those independent stores, and today some of the areas of Birmingham that once teemed with corner markets are considered food deserts. The federal government defines food deserts as areas "with limited access to affordable and nutritious food, particularly such an area composed of predominantly lower income neighborhoods and communities," which means that residents often can't get fresh, reasonably priced fruits, vegetables and other foods required for a healthy diet. Fortunately, several organizations are working to improve "food security" in these areas through initiatives such as community gardens, neighborhood farm stands and efforts to bring more fresh produce to convenience stores.

W.B. EMOND AND SON

In a 1920 *Year Book* for the Birmingham Civic Association, William B. Emond and his son, Robert, published a small ad for their grocery, calling it "the Quality Store." The line may refer both to the freshness of the food for sale and to the reputation of the Emond family, who, by that time, had been selling groceries for at least three decades.

William B. Emond appears in the city directories of the late 1880s as a clerk selling dry goods, notions, hats and hardware at various stores. These jobs may have been an apprenticeship of sorts, because in 1891, Emond opened his own store in partnership with Charles P. Owen. His choice of a grocery may have been inspired by Robert L. Emond—a

father, brother or uncle—who already operated a meat market and grocery in Elyton, a neighborhood west of downtown.

William Emond's first grocery, which also sold meats, was located on Nineteenth Street North, adjacent to the city's oldest cemetery on the edge of a growing residential area. Despite the spooky neighbors, the store was a success. Emond remained there until 1917, when he moved to the Magnolia Point building that bears his painted sign.

The collection of shops at the corner of Twenty-third Street South and Magnolia Avenue had recently been built when Emond and a son, also named Robert, opened for business. It was a promising spot, situated where a streetcar line from downtown turned to connect with a line leading to the wealthy residences on Highland Avenue and the Five

Points South commercial district. Emond also could look forward to a constant supply of customers from the lower-income white, African American and immigrant families living in the immediate neighborhood. According to a Birmingham Historical Society document, Magnolia Point's original tenants—a pharmacy, a shoe shop, ethnic groceries, meat markets and a second-floor dance hall—reflected the area's diversity. White proprietors worked next door to black proprietors, and both catered to white and black patrons.

In addition to meats, produce and other groceries, Emond and his son sold Optima Flour, which appears in a fading ad of its own below the Emonds' sign. Optima is something of a mystery, though it seems to be one of many brands of flour produced in the early part of the twentieth century. It may even have been milled in Birmingham by a company licensing the Optima name. Other painted ads for Optima Flour have been spotted as far away as Arkansas.

After seven years at Magnolia Point, the Emonds moved their grocery a few blocks to Seventh Avenue South, which was growing into a retail district. There, the store lasted another seven years and had closed by 1931. The family dwindled out of the city directories after that,

W.B. Emond and Son sold fresh meats, produce and other groceries—including Optima Flour—from a store at 2231–2235 Magnolia Avenue. The letters in the top part of the sign would have been painted a bright white or yellow on a deep black when the market opened in 1917. The Emonds moved their grocery in 1925, and about eighty years later, their faded ad gained a ghostly visitor when a graffiti artist painted phantoms on walls across the city. Jonathan Purvis.

though a John Emond continued to work as a clerk with Hill Grocery and Piggly Wiggly. If he was William's grandson or another relation, then he carried on the family tradition for a few more years.

Meanwhile, at Magnolia Point, another grocery moved in and out, later followed by a cleaners, a hat shop, a furniture store, a bar called the Dutchman and even a detective agency. Today, the building houses the offices for an art supply store.

By the early 2000s, a graffiti artist had made his own contribution to the wall below the Emond ads. Today, these painted phantoms complement one another—literal and figurative ghost signs haunting side by side.

WOODLAWN POULTRY MARKET

When the City of Birmingham annexed several surrounding municipalities in 1910, the new neighborhoods did not give up their small-town trappings. Avondale, East Lake, Ensley, North Birmingham, Pratt City, West End and Wylam retained their own central business districts, offering a convenient alternative to downtown Birmingham for local residents.

Woodlawn, a community first settled as early as 1815, had a downtown area spanning several blocks, with its own department store, cafeteria, pharmacy and even a dancing teacher. Among them was the Woodlawn Poultry Company, which moved down the street into a former auto repair garage in 1941. With few refrigerators in the home, people bought meats and other perishable foods quite often, when they were at their freshest.

You never know what you'll discover beneath old paint or siding on a Birmingham building. The owners of the structure at 6 Fifty-fifth Place North in Woodlawn found a red-and-white checkerboard façade from its days as a poultry market, from 1941 to 1959. The ad reveals how sign painters often used mortar joints as guides to keep each element, particularly lettering, even and straight. Uncovered in 2011, the fading ad now sits behind a new coat of paint, which may help preserve it for a future rediscovery. *Author's photo.*

Behind the market's red-checked façade, Emma Allen—and, later, John C. Brown Jr.—specialized in the freshest foods. What was the shopping experience like? For that, we turn to Patricia Dietlein's description of downtown Birmingham's Sanitary Market, a similar store open around the same time,

in the book *The Heritage of Jefferson County Alabama.* The small, one-room market had sawdust on the floor, she recalled. Unwrapped, unrefrigerated meats, poultry and produce were displayed in the front windows, on counters and in open crates on the floor, and a small selection of canned goods lined shelves on the walls.

The Woodlawn Poultry Company closed in 1959, a time when the one-stop shopping of supermarkets was taking customers away from smaller specialty markets. The following year, the building was converted into a tire store, and white paint concealed the colorful façade.

Today, Woodlawn is experiencing a resurgence of interest from businesses and nonprofit groups seeking to capitalize on the neighborhood's mini downtown area. In 2011, the extra paint came off the poultry market building, revealing the fading ad. By early 2012, the red checks had disappeared once again—this time concealed behind a fresh coat as the renovated building finds yet another use.

HILL GROCERY COMPANY

Hill Grocery Company did not originate in Birmingham, but it dominated the local market after its arrival in 1911. By 1932, Hill had 141 stores in the metropolitan area, mainly small, street corner locations. This one on Tuscaloosa Avenue, in the West End neighborhood of Birmingham, opened three years later, replacing an older location one block down the street. Layers of ads on the store's side wall denote this store as location no. 5, and they also highlight Fit-for-a-King coffee, "the Coffee with a Smile," a brand produced by Hill.

The Hill stores helped to popularize grocery shopping as we know it today. After opening his first store in Nashville in 1895, H.G. Hill eagerly adopted new trends such as the "cash-and-carry" concept. Originally, grocers would charge customers' purchases to credit accounts and then deliver the goods to each home. The Hill stores, like other grocers of the era, scrapped that practice in favor of encouraging customers to shop in the store, pay cash on the spot and transport their own items. The chain also was a leader in promoting itself through newspaper advertising, and it built dedicated grocery warehouses along with its own bakery to supply each store with fresh bread. A similar strategy for coffee prompted the company to acquire Fit-for-a-King and its roasting facilities early in the twentieth century.

Hill Grocery Company eventually included more than five hundred stores across the Southeast. In Birmingham, the company built a large warehouse on the Southside, connected to the railroads by a spur. However, as Hill adapted to the now commonplace self-service model of grocery shopping, in which customers collected their own items instead of having a store clerk do it for them (pioneered by the first Piggly Wiggly store, which opened in Memphis in 1916), and as supermarkets began to emerge, it consolidated smaller stores into larger locations. The Tuscaloosa Avenue corner store closed in 1952; a decade later, Winn-Dixie supermarkets purchased Hill's

At least three or four layers of ads line this wall in Birmingham's West End neighborhood, all promoting Hill Grocery Company, which moved its store no. 5 to the corner at 1101 Tuscaloosa Avenue in 1935. Fit-for-a-King coffee was one of Hill's own brands, roasted and delivered fresh to each location. Hill closed this store in 1952, and the chain left the Birmingham market ten years later. *Author's photo.*

thirty-five remaining Alabama stores. Today,
Hill continues to operate several markets in
the Nashville area.

Fit-for-a-King coffee proved to be popular
during Hill's heyday, and it may have been fit
for President Theodore Roosevelt when he
visited Nashville in 1907. After drinking a cup
of coffee at the Hermitage, Andrew Jackson's
historic home, Roosevelt declared, "This is the
kind of stuff I like to drink, by George, when
I hunt bears." The Hill company immediately
published a newspaper ad declaring that
Roosevelt had enjoyed Fit-for-a-King.
Local rival Maxwell House also claimed the
presidential endorsement for its coffee, rewriting
Roosevelt's words into its now-famous slogan,
"Good to the last drop."

Food

Birmingham's growing reputation as a town for foodies and fine dining bears no similarity to its earliest days, when the local cuisine consisted of cheap, basic grub to fuel more hours of work. Many hungry people found sustenance in the lunch counters and cook shops, often segregated by race, scattered throughout the city. A few fancier restaurants, many associated with hotels, offered more elegant dishes to the diners earning bigger paychecks.

It took Greek immigrants, who began arriving in large numbers around the turn of the twentieth century, to spice up Birmingham dining. Hundreds arrived to work in the city's iron and steel mills, but many soon discovered that they could make more money in far less dangerous professions—selling fruit and flowers, running a bootblack stand or opening a restaurant, for instance.

"Rural migrants, adjusting to a life of sidewalks, streetcars, and factory schedules, needed food in quick, accessible form," wrote Phillip Ratliff in a *Weld* article about the Greek influence on Birmingham. "Greek entrepreneurs responded by opening sandwich carts, meat-and-threes, and barbecue joints near industrial areas and working-class neighborhoods." As the city grew more prosperous, he added, the immigrants also responded to the rising demand for white-tablecloth restaurants. In each case, the Greeks brought some of the flavor of the old country to traditional southern dishes.

The local dining scene now focuses on fresh, inventive interpretations of southern cuisine that spotlight Alabama-farmed produce and meats. But Greek restaurateurs continue to operate some of the city's favorite restaurants, serving up some of the dishes that have helped to define Birmingham.

BABE'S HOT DOGS

While Birmingham chefs have won national acclaim for their culinary skills in recent decades, the city's most important—and most lasting—contribution to food culture may be its take on the humble hot dog.

Birmingham's Greek community was the driving force. Opening a hot dog stand was a relatively inexpensive proposition for newly arrived immigrants, and the city was full of workers needing a fast, cheap lunch that they

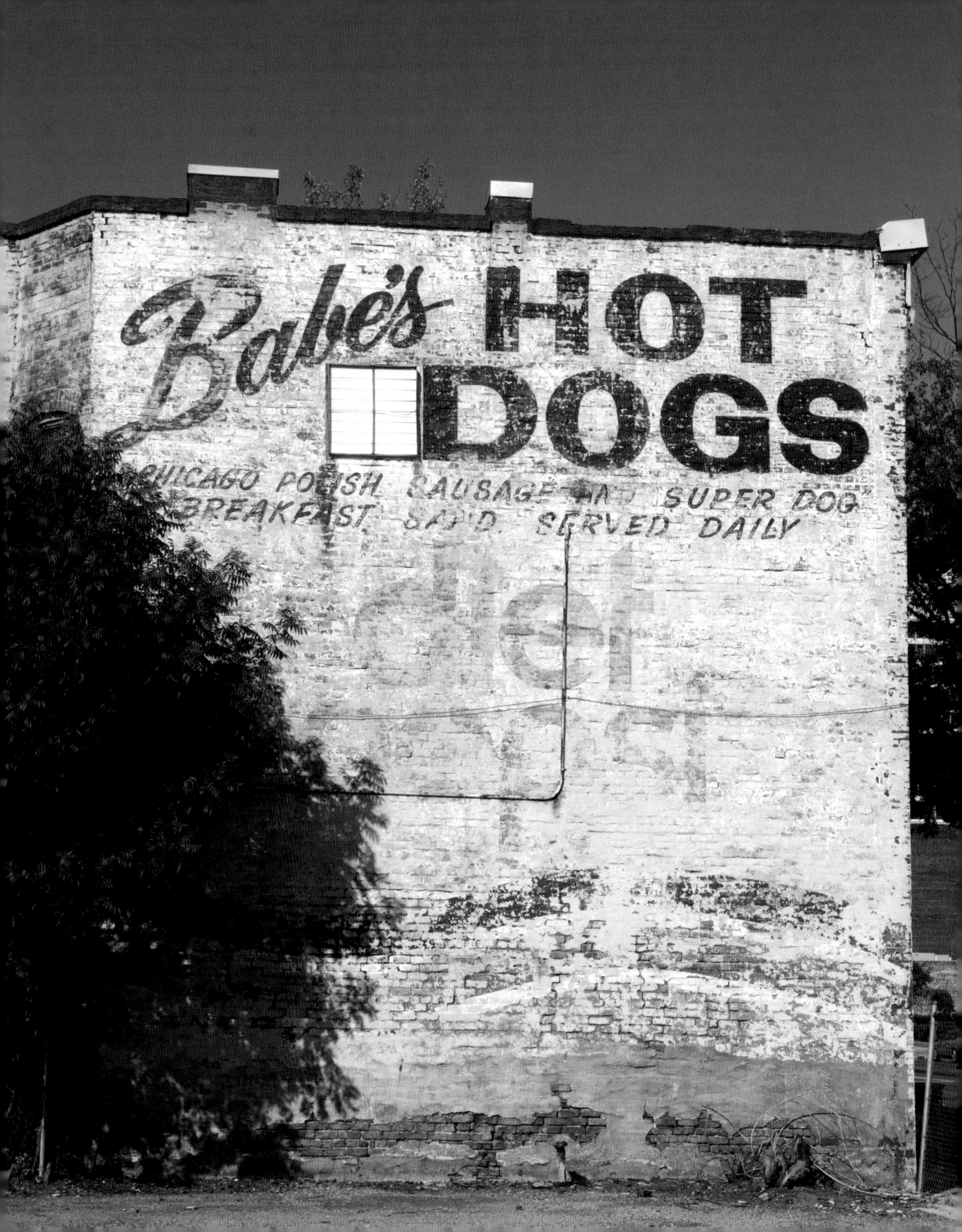
Babe's HOT
DOGS
SAUSAGE
SUPER DOG"
BREAKFAST
SERVED DAILY

could eat on the go. As they did in other local restaurants, Greek cooks added their own special flavor to a simple dish. Birmingham historian John Morse described the local hot dog as a "griddle-cooked wiener served on a slightly warmed bun topped with Greek-seasoned meat sauce, sauerkraut, onions, and mustard."

Dozens of hot dog stands populated Birmingham and its suburbs—most run by Greek families. The list has included Gus's, Sol's, Hogies, Dino's and Tony's Terrific Hot Dogs, but the most famous was the aptly named Pete's Famous Hot Dogs. Originally known as Louis's Place when Pete Koutroulakis bought the restaurant in 1939, the seven-foot-wide space became a Birmingham landmark when it was renamed Pete's Famous seven years later. And its next owner, Pete's nephew, Constantine "Gus" Koutroulakis, became a local legend for cooking hot dogs nearly every day for sixty-three years. He took over the stand after his uncle had a heart attack in 1948 and worked until the day he died in 2011, earning him a front-page obituary in the *Birmingham News*. Unfortunately, Gus's death brought an end to Pete's Famous, since he had never shared the secret recipe for his sauce.

With competition like that, Babe's Famous Hot Dogs was brave to buck the trend and offer

Babe's Famous Hot Dogs dared to take on Birmingham's traditional, Greek-inspired hot dogs with Chicago-style dogs when it opened at 1626 First Avenue North in 1985. Enough people enjoyed the Polish-sausage alternative and "Super Dog" for a second Babe's to open on Third Avenue North, but both locations had closed by 1991. *Jonathan Purvis.*

Chicago-style dogs when it opened near the corner of First Avenue North and Seventeenth Street in 1985. The Windy City's variation on the hot dog generally features sweet-pickle relish instead of Greek-style sauce, along with tomatoes, peppers, dill-pickle slices and celery salt on a poppy seed bun. (Fortunately, Babe's offered Diet Pepsi to counteract all of those delicious calories.) Its breakfast and lunch menus must have been popular because a second location of the restaurant opened on Third Avenue North in 1987.

The original Babe's stand served up its last hot dog by 1990, followed by its branch a year later. Hot dog restaurants continue to do well in Birmingham, however. Many are still owned by Greek families. And one, Sneaky Pete's (no relation to Pete's Famous), has evolved into a fast-food chain that is spreading the unique flavor of the Birmingham hot dog across northern and central Alabama.

THE BRIGHT STAR

Many people who have followed the painted star to Bessemer are on a pilgrimage of sorts—a food pilgrimage to the legendary Bright Star. The oldest restaurant in Alabama, the Bright Star is a throwback to another era, with mirrored, marbled walls; tile floors laid by hand; and murals painted by a traveling artist a century ago. In the *Birmingham News*, southern food historian John T. Edge called the Bright Star "its own kind of working man's cathedral," where anyone can dine in an elegant, inviting space alongside politicians, celebrities and college football coaches.

Diners at the Bright Star, Alabama's oldest restaurant, once parked in this lot near the corner of Bessemer's Fourth Avenue North and Nineteenth Street North. The three ads likely appeared in the 1980s, when the J.V. Davis Furniture Company began using the attached building as a warehouse. In a modern instance of the privilege system, Coca-Cola may have paid for the Bright Star's sign. Older ads for a Bruno's grocery and an auto repair shop also appear in the background, but the most intriguing is the faint figure of a boy standing to the left of the Coca-Cola logo. *Jonathan Purvis.*

The Bright Star is a Greek success story. An immigrant named Tom Bonduris opened the business as a café with twenty-five seats and a horseshoe-shaped bar in 1907, moving it to its current location by the corner of Nineteenth Street North and Third Avenue North in downtown Bessemer eight years later.

The restaurant's menu has always been a mix of Greek-seasoned dishes and southern favorites—everything from Greek-style snapper to fried green tomatoes topped with Gulf shrimp. Owned and operated by the Koikos family, relatives of Bonduris who acquired the restaurant in 1925, the Bright Star was named an "America's Classic" by the James Beard Foundation, which promotes America's culinary heritage. *Bon Appétit* magazine also has lauded it as one of America's best neighborhood restaurants.

Food pilgrims need a place to park, of course, and the painted star marks a lot on Fourth Avenue North that the restaurant, located a block away, once used. The ads fading alongside the Bright Star's sign promote Coca-Cola and the J.V. Davis Furniture Company, a Bessemer business that stored merchandise in the building behind this wall beginning in the 1980s.

Fading ads have a longer history on this wall, however. An ad identifying the lot as parking for a Bruno's grocery store on the corner—one of the early locations in the Birmingham chain that was founded in 1932 and disappeared in 2012—is visible behind the furniture sign. The cartoon of a smiling boy, perhaps the mascot of a store or product, hides just to the left of the Coca-Cola logo, and a sign underneath the Bright Star script promotes wheel alignment and brake repair for an auto shop.

Today, the parking lot seems to belong to other businesses, but foodies still flock to Bessemer to enjoy the Bright Star's classic cuisine—topped off with a slice of pineapple cheese pie.

MARY BELLE CANDIES/ OLYMPICS REAL GREEK ICES

Those with a sweet tooth will be disappointed to learn that signs are all that remains of two purveyors of sugary delights: Mary Belle Candies and Olympics Real Greek Ices. Painted on metal, the ads hang in a curious spot—in an alley between Fourth and Fifth Avenues north, where they would not have been visible to pedestrians or drivers on surrounding streets. It's possible that these signs were meant to guide delivery trucks to the back doors of the businesses. In any case, today they are most visible from a parking deck built across the alley.

Once again, a Greek family was involved in the birth of these businesses. In 1886, the Vlahos family emigrated from Greece to New Orleans. There, the family patriarch, Constantine, learned to make the city's legendary pralines, while his son sold them on the streets. Soon the family had a thriving

business, which they moved to Birmingham in 1940 and named Mary Ball Candies, after George Washington's mother.

Mary Ball's elegant Fifth Avenue North store, located at the front of this building, sold an assortment of tempting treats, including chocolates and caramels, almond pastels, bittersweet nougats, pecan rolls, English toffee, the famous pralines, a delicacy called "divine hash" and ice cream flavors such as French custard and coconut pineapple. Candies could be shipped anywhere, according to a 1955 newspaper ad. The store became a popular stop, in part because of its location next door to the La Paree steak and seafood restaurant (also Greek owned) and the original Tutwiler Hotel. Mary Ball eventually grew to include three stores in Birmingham and one each in Nashville and Atlanta.

Mary Ball became Mary Belle after the Vlahos family sold the company in 1955. By 1964, it was owned by the Manakides family and was in operation under the new name. The Mary Belle ad may have appeared at the back of the Fifth Avenue store around that time, and the passing years have revealed that its painters did a bit of recycling, using a City Federal Savings and Loan sign as their canvas. (City Federal was founded in Birmingham in 1941 and became a major player in the city's financial scene, eventually occupying the city's tallest skyscraper in the early 1960s. The company merged out of existence in 1990, but its name lives on through this fading ad and its old headquarters, now the City Federal condominiums.)

The Olympics ad appeared on the alley wall after the early 1970s, when the Manakides family was manufacturing and distributing Real Greek Ices—a semi-frozen concoction of sugar,

Painted on metal, these fading, rusting ads hide in an alley behind 2015 Fifth Avenue North. Mary Belle Candies was the successor to an elegant candy shop with a similar name, Mary Ball Candies, which was famous for its pralines, ice creams and other sweet delights. The Mary Belle ad, painted over an older sign for City Federal Savings and Loan, went up after 1964, when the shop's new owners changed the name. The colorful ad for Olympics Real Greek Ices followed in the late 1970s with a switch to European-style semi-frozen treats. That version of the store lasted three years. *Jonathan Purvis.*

water and flavorings much like Italian granitas. After Mary Belle closed in 1979, Olympics occupied the Fifth Avenue space for three more years. A succession of short-lived restaurants followed, and today the storefront sits vacant like an empty chocolate box, tempting us with what once was there.

STULL'S HIGHLAND ICE CREAM/BARBER DAIRIES

The passage of decades can do nothing to dull the memory of a delicious scoop of ice cream. Though Birmingham's small, homegrown dairies are long gone, their customers still can recall the delicious details of their favorite flavors and the joyous experiences of getting a cone, milkshake or sundae.

One of those local dairies, Stull's Highland Ice Cream, won fans with flavors such as cherry vanilla, black walnut, butter pecan, vanilla bonbon, caramel, lemon and fudge royal. Its namesake, David L. Stull, had run an ice cream parlor in Altoona, Pennsylvania, before moving to Birmingham in about 1910. Once here, he helped to organize the Birmingham Ice Cream Company ("makers of Worthmore Ice Cream"), and in about 1925, he became owner of the Highland Ice Cream Company, located on Seventh Avenue South.

Ice cream had been a popular treat in Birmingham since at least 1898, when three parlors opened in the city. By 1900, a dedicated ice cream manufacturing company had joined the many local dairies. The ice cream cone itself had become a hit at the 1904 St. Louis World's Fair—the same exposition where Birmingham's iconic *Vulcan* statue first wowed crowds in the city's exhibit. Ice cream makers could count on Alabama's hot summers to help drive sales, but they also benefited from local and national prohibition laws, when saloons had to seek alternative attractions for their customers.

David Stull did more than scoop up ice cream, however. He also was an inventor who developed new technologies for manufacturing ice cream. In 1923, he received a patent for a cone-baking machine, and according to his hometown newspaper in Altoona, it could bake cones "over four times as fast as any known machine." It also reported that Stull "has refused several handsome offers for his patent."

Stull also patented an ice cream freezer in 1936, with Mercer David Grayson listed as joint inventor. The next year, Grayson became a competitor, founding Grayson's Delicious Ice Creams. The company eventually had multiple locations in Birmingham and became known for its Spinning Wheel milkshakes, as well as its drive-in on First Avenue North that was covered in a concrete snowscape, complete with icicles and a polar bear on the roof.

After Stull's death in 1942, the Stull's Highland Ice Cream Company was formed, eventually marketing its ice creams to other parlors, including the Highland Bakery on Nineteenth Street South in Bessemer. The Hannah family operated the store, which opened in the 1930s and enticed generations of customers with its doughnuts, cinnamon rolls, wedding cakes and other fresh-from-the-oven delights. But ice cream was a main draw. On a Facebook page for the Bessemer Hall of History, former customers recall visiting Highland Bakery for a couple of scoops of Stull's. More

For sixty years, Highland Bakery, located at 10 Nineteenth Street South in Bessemer, was a popular stop for cinnamon rolls, doughnuts and ice cream especially. The preferred scoops came from Stull's Highland, named for a local ice cream mogul who invented both ice cream machines and delicious flavors. The ad on the side of the former bakery dates from the 1970s, when Birmingham's Barber Dairies acquired the Stull's brand. *Jonathan Purvis.*

than one commenter called that ice cream the best they had ever tasted.

Barber Dairies, the other company featured on the bakery's ad, was founded by George H. Barber in Birmingham in the early 1930s. With its own ice plant, the dairy could keep its products cold in delivery trucks, helping them to stay fresh all the way to customers' houses. Barber and his company became advocates for milk pasteurization regulations and new forms of packaging—such as the now familiar milk carton and white plastic jug—and expanded its offerings to include ice cream, butter, cottage cheese, sour cream and other dairy products.

Over the decades, Barber grew into a regional dairy producer and processor, in part through acquisitions of smaller dairies—including Stull's Highland Ice Cream, which merged with Barber in 1972. The fading ad on the side of Highland Bakery may date from that time, since it features both the Stull's and Barber brands. Eventually, the dairy stopped using the Stull's name in favor of promoting Barber's own ice cream line.

Today, Barber carries the title of Alabama's oldest dairy, and before the Barber family sold the company in 1998, it distributed milk in five states and ice cream in twenty-five states and also had operations in Puerto Rico and Chile. As for Highland Bakery, it brought its last cookies and cinnamon rolls out of the oven in the early 1990s, and now its building stands empty, leaving behind a fading ad that has been known to trigger a sudden hankering for a scoop of cherry vanilla.

Retail

Although Twentieth Street has always served as Birmingham's main street, running from Red Mountain to Linn Park, the main retail district gravitated just to the west, settling in the blocks surrounding Nineteenth Street.

The stores began small, offering general merchandise or dry goods, clothing, hardware and agricultural items to serve the area's rural population. But as the little town of Birmingham grew into a big city, the retailers got larger and more specialized.

Inspired by department stores in cities like Chicago, hometown favorites Pizitz, Loveman's and Saks built ornate multistory buildings that dominated the area. They were joined by national chains such as Kress and Woolworth, which constructed their own retail palaces. A mix of shops and smaller department stores—Blach's, Parisian, Burger-Phillips, New Ideal and New Williams among them—filled the spaces in between, along with restaurants and theaters.

The streets hummed with activity. In the early twentieth century, locals cruised a route known as "the Racetrack," making a loop of the area on Nineteenth Street, Third Avenue North, Twentieth Street and Second Avenue North. "People and automobiles went round

and round, chatting, courting, and enjoying the life of the downtown, big-city shopping streets," wrote Marjorie White in *Downtown Birmingham: Architectural and Historical Walking Tour Guide*. During the holidays, each of the big department stores tried to outdo its rivals with elaborate show windows and, in the case of Pizitz, an entire animated Enchanted Forest inside the building.

The retail district's energetic atmosphere—and the crowds of eager buyers—didn't change much until shopping centers began popping up in Birmingham's suburbs. Many downtown department stores and national retailers opened branches in the new developments, offering a convenient, close-to-home alternative for busy shoppers. In 1960, Eastwood Mall, the first enclosed mall in the Deep South, opened for business on Birmingham's east side. Once shoppers got a glimpse of "the Merchandise City of the Future" and felt the air conditioning on the avenue linking its forty stores, they were hooked. Suddenly the locals had a new place to cruise.

Many of the downtown stores eventually closed. The iconic hometown department stores vanished altogether, many in mergers with out-of-state retailers; others simply went out of business after a century or more of service. Some of the buildings they left behind might open their doors once more, however. Developers have been looking at several of the empty storefronts around the old Racetrack, envisioning the wide-open sales floors as future space for offices, housing and, most fittingly, new retail.

LOUIS SAKS CLOTHIERS

A century ago, a plain, white-on-black ad directed shoppers to one of Birmingham's most fashionable corners. "Saks" was Louis Saks Clothiers, a department store that sold "everything in stylish, ready-to-wear apparel for men, women and children at lowest prices consistent with high quality," according to a 1907 advertisement.

Louis Saks was a prominent Jewish merchant, born in Germany, who came to Birmingham in 1884 to open his store. Eleven years later, he constructed this three-story building on one of the city's busiest corners. In addition to the sign on the store's east wall, "Clothiers for the Whole Family" was painted between the second and third floors on the Nineteenth Street façade.

Saks was a frequent advertiser in the city's newspapers, but in 1899, he jumped at the opportunity for some cheap publicity. On June 1, an Anti-Spitting Law went into effect, imposing fines between one dollar and five dollars on anyone "convicted of spitting on the sidewalks, in street cars, in public buildings and churches of this city." Immediately,

Saks ordered large spittoons—each two feet wide and one foot high—to be placed on street corners at major intersections. The gaudily painted spittoons carried the slogan, "We provide for the Public. Louis Saks, the clothier." According to one account, Saks's response to the controversial law became a hot topic itself, being "commented upon by hundreds daily."

A fire sparked by a live wire heavily damaged the Saks building in 1910, causing an estimated loss of $240,000. Saks held a "fire sale" and then rebuilt the store, but six years later, he constructed a new, five-story building one block away—directly between his biggest retailing rivals, the Pizitz and Loveman, Joseph and Loeb department stores. Saks retired from business in 1933 and died in 1942. His store changed owners and names, becoming Melancon's and later a J.J. Newberry's variety store.

The original Saks building became home to a drugstore, a jeweler and multiple clothing stores. It was renovated in 1984, and today it houses a nonprofit organization devoted to promoting child care. The formerly bold Saks sign now looks smudged.

Though Louis Saks was not affiliated with the Saks Fifth Avenue chain, Birmingham briefly

In 1895, Louis Saks Clothiers, one of Birmingham's leading department stores, staked its claim to the corner of First Avenue North and Nineteenth Street with a bold "SAKS" painted on the side of its new emporium. At least two versions of the ad—one with block lettering and another with a more elegant style—appeared here. The former flagship store for Pizitz, a Saks competitor, stands in the background. *Jonathan Purvis.*

A photo from about 1910 shows the Saks ad in its prime and highlights the importance of the store's address. Both the twin-towered Morris Hotel and the new chamber of commerce building (now Jemison Flats) shared the intersection with Saks and faced its main entrance. *Birmingham, Alabama, Public Library Archives, file #1556.29.88.*

served as headquarters for the iconic New York retailer. In 1997, the Proffitt's department store chain of Knoxville, Tennessee, moved its headquarters to Alabama after purchasing Birmingham's Parisian stores. A year later, it acquired the holding company for Saks Fifth Avenue and became one of the nation's largest department store operators. Renamed Saks Inc., the company eventually sold off its other department stores and relocated to Manhattan in 2007.

New Ideal

With a name that sounds as optimistic as "New Ideal," it's no wonder the department store painted it twenty-one times on its façade. But why do all of these ads appear on the *back* wall, facing an alley?

The best guess is that the store used the signs to attract shoppers headed for its bigger rival, Pizitz. For many years, Pizitz had used the corner of the block behind New Ideal as a parking lot; in 1965, it opened a seven-story parking deck on the site, connecting it to the store with an enclosed skyway. The painted words would have demanded the attention of anyone in the parking lot and would flash by as drivers circled the lower levels of the deck, serving as a reminder to add New Ideal to a shopping trip. Alerting customers to the New Ideal's location may have been important because the store had already held multiple downtown addresses since its founding in 1908, and no retailer wants a prospective customer peering into an empty storefront.

The store's previous home was a six-story building built in about 1928 on Nineteenth Street. Then it was known simply as the Ideal Department Store, and the design of the new store lived up to its slogan of "Built on Better Values." Its owners, the Aland family, hired the architect responsible for the Thomas Jefferson Hotel to create a showpiece, with an intricate terra-cotta façade and Italian marble tile in the lobby.

Just six years later, however, the Ideal moved a few streets over to a prime spot on Second Avenue North between Pizitz and Sears, which held down the corners of the 1800 block. The store was renamed the New Ideal to highlight the new address, and it retained that name when it relocated yet again. In 1941, the New Ideal moved into the Sears space at the corner of Second and Eighteenth Street when that department store left for its sprawling new complex farther down the street. The painted signs on the back wall, along with a landmark neon sign highlighting the New Ideal name on the corner, appeared sometime afterward.

A rhyming newspaper ad from the early 1970s describes the New Ideal's merchandise as fashions for "the teens and the tots, the infants, grandmothers…The misses, the chubbies, the sons, and the brothers." The downtown store remained in business until about 1990 and has been empty since then. In recent years, the New Ideal building has been slated for redevelopment into street-level retail and restaurants, with office space or loft apartments on the upper floors.

After rival Pizitz opened a giant parking deck in 1965, the New Ideal Department Store reminded shoppers of its existence by painting its name twenty-one times on its back wall—right where people could see it as they arrived at the larger store. Both downtown retailers survived until the end of the 1980s, with Pizitz—by then a McRae's—shutting down a year or two before New Ideal closed for good. Jonathan Purvis.

KESSLER'S

Many of Birmingham's prominent Jewish merchants began their careers in small towns, running dry goods stores and similar businesses before setting out for the big city. But Adolph Kessler Sr. took the opposite route, starting out big in New York, where he was a stylist and designer for the Bonwit-Teller department store.

Kessler arrived in Birmingham in about 1913, the year he is listed in city directories as a tailor for the Louis Saks department store. Within a few years, however, he had partnered with Benjamin Sherer to open a store on Third Avenue North selling ready-to-wear fashions for women.

By 1937, Kessler had moved his store down the street into a larger structure—an 1890 edifice that had already housed a produce seller, a parade of shoe stores, a jeweler and a hosiery shop. The new address placed Kessler's women's wear store on one of Birmingham's busiest shopping blocks, directly between two heavyweights of Birmingham retail—the Blach's and Burger-Phillips department stores.

The Kessler's ad appears in a photo of Third Avenue North from the 1950s, but the first version of the sign may have been painted earlier. Recent weathering reveals that it was painted over at least one other sign advertising a photo studio located on the same block.

Adolph Kessler's store for women moved to 1924–1926 Third Avenue North in 1937, and the first ad bearing his scripted name showed up by the 1950s. As the paint has faded, older signs have reemerged. The faint "photo studio" ad could refer to nearly half a dozen photographers located along this block in the 1910s and 1920s, but it most likely belonged to H.T. Morton, whose studio was in the building directly underneath the sign in 1917. *Jonathan Purvis.*

Adolph's three sons had joined the business by 1959, when the family began a $50,000 renovation of the store and laid plans for expansion. Changes included a new Third Avenue entrance featuring dramatic curving show windows and a polished pink and black granite floor with a spiral design mirroring one on the ceiling. A *Birmingham News* article quoting the Kessler brothers notes that behind-the-scenes upgrades included "new photostatic machines which will enable bookkeepers to mail copies of original sales slips along with statements to customers." We can assume that those shoppers found the spiral floor more dazzling.

Kessler's had also begun opening suburban branches in the 1950s, and eventually these eclipsed the downtown store, which closed by 1986. The last Kessler's store, located in Vestavia Hills, was shut down in 1995 after the death of Abraham Kessler, one of Adolph's sons. In the late 2000s, the downtown building was renovated into loft apartments, preserving the spiral entranceway and a bit of Adolph's New York style.

YEILDING'S

Just how friendly was "your friendly department store"? A local legend says that Yeilding's moved several blocks from its original location on Twentieth Street—a prime spot in the middle of downtown—because the electric streetcars spooked the customers' horses.

The store wanted to keep horses—but especially their farmer owners—happy because they had been a key target market since

Yeilding's opened in 1876. Founded by William Hood, who was joined the next year by his brother-in-law, Frank B. Yeilding, the general merchandise store sold plows, wagons, seed, fertilizer, hardware, groceries and clothing, among other necessities. The store, then known as Hood-Yeilding and Company, was located on Twentieth Street in the heart of the city. (The building later became Blach's department store, now the Blach's Lofts.) Frank and his brother, William, eventually purchased the store from Hood, changing the name to Yeilding Brothers Company.

Yeilding's moved to the streetcar-free corner of Second Avenue North and Twenty-second Street in 1911. The new three-story department store included a grocery, as well as a boardinghouse on the second floor. This location became the flagship store as the company's focus narrowed to men's and women's clothing and as it grew into one of Birmingham's major retailers.

Figuring out when the Yeilding's signs appeared on the building's rear façade is complicated because the expansive brick wall has hosted a series of painted ads. A close inspection reveals traces of the words "Baking," "Cake" and "Butter" in the beige paint from an early mural. By the late 1910s or early 1920s, they had been covered by a colorful ad for Snowdrift, "the perfect shortening," that stretched two and a half stories up the wall. Used for making cakes, breads, pastries and fried foods, Snowdrift debuted as the first fully vegetable oil shortening at the turn of the twentieth century—at the time, it was considered a cheaper alternative to lard. The nationally distributed *Snowdrift Secrets* cookbook from 1913 called it a "pure and clean" product endorsed by physicians that was economical because it could

Yeilding's was one of Birmingham's oldest department stores, originating as a farm-focused retailer in 1876. Its flagship store at the intersection of Second Avenue North and Twenty-second Street opened in 1911, and its large back wall became a canvas for ads. Words from a Snowdrift shortening ad, painted in about 1920, are visible on the right. The two Yeilding's signs followed a few decades later. *Jonathan Purvis.*

be "used over and over again for frying different things, as it will not absorb the odor or taste of foods fried in it."

The Yeilding's ads probably were painted in the 1940s, 1950s or 1960s, and they served, in part, as directional signs because both are visible from the well-traveled First Avenue North. At its peak, the family-owned company operated seven stores in metropolitan Birmingham and another in Huntsville. By the 1990s, Yeilding's was selling only women's clothing, but increased competition forced the company to close all of its stores in 1996 after 120 years in business. The downtown location had been shuttered in 1980, and today it remains vacant, once again offering a quiet corner for any nervous horses that might amble through the neighborhood.

DIXIE CYCLE AND TOY/COOK CREDIT FURNITURE

Traces of Dixie Cycle and Toy Company are tough to find—except in the memories of the children who discovered wheeled freedom in its aisles.

"The whole place smelled like rubber," recalled writer David Pelfrey, who grew up in Birmingham. "It didn't have the brake fluid aroma you would get at Western Auto, so we liked Dixie Cycle and Toy a little better."

The shop originally opened in 1953 on Second Avenue North, a few streets away from where its painted ad now sits—just in time to serve a generation of young baby boomers. "Almost everyone I knew as a very little kid had a Radio Flyer something or other, or a tricycle, from that store," Pelfrey said. A 1957 telephone directory listing notes that the store specialized in "nationally advertised bicycles" along with parts, tires and, of course, toys. It was one of fifteen independent bike shops in the metropolitan area at the time.

Dixie Cycle moved to 1711 First Avenue North in about 1976, but the signs didn't

Dixie Cycle and Toy Company and Cook Credit Furniture painted signs at 1711 First Avenue North in the 1980s, contributing to a collection of wall ads that stretches back to the early twentieth century. The two newer ads are unusual in that they resemble a freestanding billboard. *Jonathan Purvis.*

appear until at least a decade later, when Cook Credit Furniture partnered on the paint job. Located a couple of streets over at 1717 Third Avenue North, Cook began as a loan and sales company on a block full of loan offices and furniture stores in 1985. The city directory for the following year lists the company as Cook Credit Furniture. The firm later became Cook Finance Company before closing down by 1990.

Dixie and Cook painted their signs on the side of the Dixie building on First Avenue North, atop already fading ads for Uneeda Biscuit and Bull Durham. Curiously, the Cook ad, tempting drivers to turn the corner and find out how to score a free rabbit-eared TV, resembles a billboard—complete with the illustration of a support structure. While it seems ironic that the painted ad looks like the very medium that was replacing paint, that was not a new idea. In fact, photographs of Birmingham streets from the end of the 1930s show painted ads for shortening and soft drinks in illustrated frames that mimic the real ones surrounding billboards at the time. The real irony is that actual billboards once covered the section of wall where the Dixie and Cook ads were painted, according to a photograph from the Birmingham Public Library Archives. In this case at least, paint replaced billboards.

Dixie Cycle and Toy changed its merchandise mix over time, becoming Dixie Fitness in the early 1990s. The store remained at its First Avenue location until rolling out for good in 1996, leaving behind its ad and the rubbery whiff of nostalgia for generations of grown-up children.

JEFFERSON HOME FURNITURE

Furniture stores have been a mainstay of downtown Birmingham for more than 130 years. The 1883–84 city directory lists five of them, and it seems that most of them made their own pieces. (One business belonging to E. Erswell lists furniture, upholstery and undertaking among his specialties.) The most impressive early store might have been Peter Zinszer's Mammoth Furniture House, which opened on Second Avenue North in 1889. Behind a highly ornamented cast-iron and glass façade, Zinszer offered customers four floors of home furnishings, including a plethora of carpets and stoves.

In the following decades, furniture stores blossomed on nearly every downtown block. Big names included Calder, Haverty, Marks Fitzgerald, Hood-McPherson, Hunter, Spencer, Standard and Rhodes-Carroll, to name just a few. Even in 1937, in the heart of the Great Depression, Birmingham boasted more than seventy furniture stores, with a majority clustered downtown.

Many of these stores marked their locations with large painted signs displaying their names to be seen blocks away, but the largest belonged to Jefferson Home Furniture. Nathan Rotenstreich founded the company in 1932, and by 1965, it had moved into a six-story building and neighboring smaller structure at 1716–18 Second Avenue North. The taller building, constructed in 1925, had already housed a variety of furniture stores, beginning with the J.E. Cain Company. Another early tenant was a dancing school on the top floor. The smaller building next door was built in

Jefferson Home Furniture moved to 1716–1718 Second Avenue North around 1965 and painted several layers of ads on its eastern wall, some of which are partially legible. Higher up, the signs promoted free parking, a handy benefit to offer shoppers used to the convenience of suburban retail centers. *Jonathan Purvis.*

in 1997. In the past decade, its two buildings were slated to become the Jefferson Lofts, with a penthouse in the former dance studio, but the economic downturn of the late 2000s put those plans on hold.

about 1915 and was the location for Excelsior Laundry and—yes—more furniture stores over the years. Jefferson Home painted several layers of ads on the exposed side wall of the smaller structure. Other signs, painted near the roofline of the higher building, pointed to the store and its parking lot.

The company grew into a chain of ten stores across north Alabama before closing

STORKLAND BABY FURNITURE

In the 1950s, Birmingham instituted a series of one-way streets to funnel heavy volumes of traffic into and out of downtown. Two decades later, Storkland, a retailer of baby furniture, took full advantage of the change by painting the back wall of its building with an ad for the

store—alongside an ad for Coca-Cola (which might have paid for the prominent wall space). No one could drive Twenty-second Street, a one-way heading south, without noticing the brightly painted double ads among the brick buildings.

Both ads were probably painted after 1976–77, when Storkland opened on the corner of Twenty-second and First Avenue North. Its home had been a prized location since it was built in the early 1910s, when First Avenue was developing into one of the city's main streets. For many years, the second floor was the headquarters for the Alabama Engraving Company, which made artwork for printed publications. (The company's name and "makers of Printwell Plates" can still be seen in a faint ad on the building's west side.) The first floor housed a series of Greek-owned confectioners and restaurants in its early days—including the offices of the "Banana King" of Birmingham, Alex Kontos, who made a fortune in the fruit wholesale business. Later, the space welcomed a barber, a tobacco wholesaler, a dictating machine company, a bakery and a jeweler, among other businesses.

Though Storkland Baby Furniture moved out of downtown Birmingham in the 1990s, its large ad—and an impressionistic Coke counterpart—continues to draw attention. Both signs went up in about 1976–77, when Storkland opened at the corner of First Avenue North and Twenty-second Street. According to the ad, the baby store sold layettes, linen, gifts and toys in addition to furniture. *Jonathan Purvis.*

Storkland had originated in Vestavia Hills a few years before opening downtown. Following its move to First Avenue, the furniture store remained in the space for twenty years, eventually sharing it with a supplier of uniforms. Today, Storkland continues to outfit nurseries from a location in Vestavia Hills and a downtown clearance center.

As for Storkland's former building, it was considered for a loft development but now houses a private residence on the second floor. And the ads on the back wall are still doing their job, drawing the attention of drivers heading one way out of downtown.

ALABAMA STORE FIXTURE COMPANY/DIXIE STORE FIXTURES

A few blocks east of Birmingham's main retail district, a cluster of businesses sprang up to provide shopkeepers with the perfect platforms to display their wares.

Alabama Store Fixture Company was one of them, selling a variety of racks and glass showcases, and possibly even mannequins and window dressings like some of its competitors. Located on the first floor of the former rooming house at 112 Twenty-fourth Street North (see the chapter on Places to Stay), the store's large painted sign was designed to catch the attention of potential customers on First Avenue North. No doubt they also saw the large Pepsi logo that was part of the ad. As we have seen before, the soda company probably paid Alabama Store Fixture for the right to use the wall and might have even funded the entire sign.

Above: Dixie Store Fixtures supplies equipment to restaurants and other food service providers, so it's fitting that its headquarters at 2425 First Avenue North once housed a baking company. Fading ads for Martin Biscuit Company cookies and other products, made there from 1910 to 1928, still line the building's west side. Dixie added its own signs after it relocated to the space in the 1960s. *Jonathan Purvis.*

Below: The storefront at 112 Twenty-fourth Street North has housed a variety of businesses over more than a century, but in 1984, it welcomed Alabama Store Fixture Company, which featured a large Pepsi logo in its wall ad visible from First Avenue North. Despite that big splash, the company stayed downtown just two years. *Jonathan Purvis.*

Alabama Store Fixture was a young company when it relocated to Twenty-fourth Street in 1984, and it stayed there only two years before moving to the east side of Birmingham. In contrast, Dixie Store Fixtures, located a few blocks away, has been a mainstay of downtown Birmingham since 1921. Founded by Joe and Pearl Cypress, the company originally supplied equipment mainly to drugstores; later, it expanded to service restaurants.

After Dixie moved to its current location on First Avenue North in the 1960s, it painted its own ads atop those for the Martin Biscuit Company, headquartered in the building from about 1910 until it built a new plant in Lakeview in 1928. Founded by Birmingham bakery salesman Edgar Martin, the firm produced Marco brand crackers, cakes, Milk and Honey cookies, vanilla wafers, ginger snaps and moon pies that were sold throughout the South. For a time, the company also distributed candy. Painted illustrations of Martin's baked goods once decorated the wall, leaving behind faint shapes that are visible next to the Dixie sign.

Today, Dixie continues to be owned and operated by its founding family. Its customer base has grown beyond restaurants, however, and now includes clients as diverse as hospitals and sports stadiums.

Industry

Birmingham owes its existence to a stroke of geologic luck. The area surrounding Jones Valley contains all of the key ingredients for cooking up steel: iron ore, coal and limestone. (A painted ad on the back of the Lincoln Life building—now Jemison Flats—in downtown Birmingham once proclaimed that all three could be found within the range of a gunshot.)

Though a few mines and foundries dotted the area before the Civil War, exploitation of the district's mineral resources didn't really begin until two railroads—the Alabama & Chattanooga and the South & North—began making their way through the area. The Elyton Land Company seized the opportunity to build an industrial city where the lines crossed.

Birmingham's iron boom really began in 1880, when the Alice Furnace, located on the city's western edge (about where Interstate 65 rolls through today), began operating. It proved that pig iron could be produced at a cheaper cost here than anywhere else in the United States. More furnaces followed, and "by 1898, the city was considered to be the third-largest point of pig iron export in the world," after Middlesbrough, England, and

Glasgow, Scotland, according to Marjorie White in *The Birmingham District: An Industrial History and Guide*.

The boom also brought factories that turned the pig iron into products. Rolling mills, which flattened iron into sheets or formed it into other shapes, occupied parts of Birmingham's Southside. Other plants turned metal into stoves, radiators, steam engines, architectural elements and machine parts. Birmingham became the nation's capital of cast-iron pipe. Steel production began in the area in 1897, launching an entire new industry. Birmingham companies used local steel to produce railcars, as well as beams, rivets and plates used in bridges, buildings and even ships in the United States and internationally.

Nine rail lines eventually made their way through Birmingham, making it a prime place to manufacture and distribute any kind of product. By the 1920s, local factories churned out brick, cement, lumber, cotton gins and textiles.

The Great Depression took a heavy toll on Birmingham industry, which recovered with the increased demand for steel brought by World War II. In the ensuing decades, however, rising production costs and foreign competition led to a decline in a variety of industries, particularly iron, steel and mining.

Though many factories and mines closed between the 1950s and 1970s, Birmingham remains a major industrial center and continues to manufacture steel, cast-iron pipe and construction materials, among other products.

Sloss Furnaces

The smokestacks of Sloss Furnaces loom large on Birmingham's skyline and in its history. James Withers Sloss, a merchant and plantation owner who helped to bring the railroad to Jones Valley, opened his blast furnace for making iron in 1882 on what was then the city's outskirts. It was the second of nineteen furnaces built during Jefferson County's 1880s iron boom, and it became one of the most successful.

By the early 1900s, the company—then known as Sloss-Sheffield Steel and Iron—owned seven blast furnaces, 1,500 ovens for turning coal into coke (a carbon material used in ironmaking), multiple coal and ore mines, quarries, 120,000 acres of land and 1,200 houses for its workers. Before World War I, Sloss-Sheffield was one of the world's largest producers of pig iron, so called because the molten metal flowed into branching channels in a way that brought to mind a sow with suckling piglets. (The resulting iron bars are called "pigs.") The company shipped the iron bars across the South and Midwest to be melted down and formed into pipe, stoves and many other products.

With all of that metal in motion around Sloss Furnaces, the ads painted on the old coke bin illustrate an interesting historical footnote: at one time, Sloss also manufactured motor fuel, concrete and even bug spray. Karen Utz, curator for Sloss Furnaces, explained that the company transformed the byproducts of ironmaking into entirely new goods that boosted the bottom line when demand for pig iron was low. The petrochemical benzene, for example, was converted into Sloss Special Benzol, "the perfect motor fuel." Slag, a rocky-looking waste product, was recycled for concrete. The coke-making process generated xylol, a chemical that became the DeaDinsecT pesticide. (It also contained DDT, naturally.) Other products included aluminum paint and mineral wool.

Richard Neely, PhD, a history professor and Sloss Furnaces volunteer, said that ads for Sloss products had been painted on the coke bin wall at least two or three times, likely beginning in the 1920s or 1930s. He and his brother, John Neely, restored the last batch of ads in 1998–99, using old photographs and the fading letters and shapes as guides.

In the decades after World War II, international competition, technological changes and a growing focus on reducing air pollution battered Birmingham's iron and steel industry. U.S. Pipe, which had merged with Sloss-Sheffield, closed the downtown furnaces in 1970, and they were nearly demolished until a public outcry saved them. In 1983, the partially restored complex was reopened to the public. Today, the Sloss Furnaces National Historic Landmark is "currently the only twentieth-century blast furnace plant in the nation being preserved and interpreted as an

Not many people realize that Sloss Furnaces, an icon of Birmingham's iron age, also made motor fuel, paint, concrete and insect-killing DDT from its byproducts. Ads for Sloss-branded goods began appearing on this wall at the plant by the 1920s or 1930s. Richard and John Neely restored them in 1998–99 with the same type of oil-based industrial paints that the original artists used. *Jonathan Purvis.*

industrial museum," Utz said. The Sloss site also attracts visitors with concerts, barbecue and beer festivals and even performances of Shakespeare. And in a nod to the site's history, a metal arts program has reinvigorated one of the old casting sheds, enabling artists and visitors to discover the creative uses of molten iron.

YOUNG AND VANN SUPPLY COMPANY

Entrepreneurs I.F. Young and James A. Vann began a partnership in 1906 to supply blast furnaces, mines and rolling mills with hardware. Within six years, their company had grown so fast that it needed a new home, and they found an unlikely landlord.

In 1888, Anheuser-Busch constructed a two-story beer distribution warehouse—one of only six in the country—on the corner of Morris Avenue and Eighteenth Street, right next to the railroad tracks that run through the center of Birmingham. Large arched doorways enabled horses to pull wagons full of beer from

The Young and Vann Supply Company moved into a former beer warehouse at the corner of First Avenue North and Eighteenth Street in about 1912. The words on the Morris Avenue side of the building date from a decade or two later, when Young and Vann had expanded beyond its original focus on hardware for mines and mills to offer belts, hoses, pipes and rope, among other items. *Jonathan Purvis.*

the railroad directly into the warehouse. A few years later, the brewer added a three-story office building to connect with the First Avenue North side of the block.

But Anheuser-Busch had moved on by 1912, and the Young and Vann Company saw the building as the perfect location for its offices and storage. After leasing the building for many years, Young and Vann purchased it in 1925. By then, the company had expanded beyond its original customer base and was a distributor of industrial supplies to customers throughout the Southeast. Its *Red Book* catalogue contained

hardware such as roofing, paints, tools and even lawnmowers, garden hoses and wheelbarrows.

The back wall of the headquarters building served as another kind of catalogue. Young and Vann's fading ad lists key items in the firm's inventory, including packing (sealing materials), belts, hoses, pumps, rope and pipe measuring up to two feet in diameter. The "sketch" among them relates to pipe fitting, which requires a technical drawing to determine what pipes are needed and where they fit into a building plan.

Turner Supply Company of Mobile acquired Young and Vann in 2000. Four years later, the former headquarters building reopened as the Center for Regional Planning and Design, housing the Regional Planning Commission of Greater Birmingham, the Auburn University Center for Architecture and Urban Studies (also known as the Urban Studio), the Cultural Alliance of Greater Birmingham, the Birmingham History Center, an art gallery and other community-focused organizations. One piece of hardware was left behind, however. A large floor scale that once weighed freight now stands in an office space as a reminder of Young and Vann's contributions to the growth of heavy industry in Birmingham.

THE GEORGE F. WHEELOCK COMPANY

Birmingham's rapid population growth in the 1880s, the decade when many of the blast furnaces started production, prompted a building boom. New houses, stores, hotels, schools, churches, public buildings and other structures filled in the blocks of the city plan. These buildings were functional, but they didn't skimp on the architectural flourishes that mark the Victorian era.

According to Marjorie White's *Downtown Birmingham: Architectural and Historical Walking Tour Guide*, Birmingham construction at that time displayed "considerable refinement" because the developing city drew young architects, contractors and builders possessing both talent and ambition. Among them was George F. Wheelock, who arrived from New York State in 1888. He set up a shop at 109 Richard Arrington Jr. Boulevard (then Twenty-first Street South) to manufacture architectural elements out of sheet metal—a common building material for Victorian structures.

The oldest ad on the side of the former George F. Wheelock Company building, constructed in about 1888 at 109 Richard Arrington Jr. Boulevard South, lists the firm's specialties, including roofing, furnaces and sheet metal. Below it, a company logo resembles letterhead used around the time that Wheelock moved to a new location in the 1920s. Traces of an early Pepsi-Cola ad also are visible. *Author's photo.*

Products included window caps, skylights and galvanized roof cornices, which gave buildings a decorative roofline and also provided walls with some protection from the weather. Wheelock could point to the elaborate cornice topping his own building as proof of what his company could do.

The firm changed its business model over the years, evolving into a roofing and sheet metal contractor for clients throughout the Southeast and then adding furnaces for residential and commercial construction. To promote itself, Wheelock painted ads on the north and south façades of its Twenty-first Street building that would have demanded the attention of anyone using the route to and from downtown Birmingham. At least two layers of faint ads decorate the southern side, listing services—roofing, furnaces and sheet metal work—and the Wheelock name in a typeface used by the company in the 1920s. The partially obscured ad on the opposite side of the building simply spells out the company name in giant block letters.

The high visibility of the Wheelock building also made it a magnet for soft drink advertising. The outlines of a painted Pepsi-Cola ad from about 1907 remain at street level on the southern side of the building, and around the same time, a two-story-tall red Coca-Cola ad dominated the northern façade just below the black-and-white Wheelock sign. The Coke ad now hides behind the brick walls of an adjacent building.

All of the ads on the building predate 1927, when the George F. Wheelock Company moved to another location in town. The company remains at that address and continues to do business as a wholesale distributor of heating, ventilation and air conditioning products. Over the decades, the original headquarters housed a supplier of X-ray machines and an art gallery, among other tenants, and it endured multiple rounds of renovation. The Victorian cornice came down in one of those modernizations, leaving the fading ads as the building's only visible link to its past.

The Automotive District

Birmingham has a love affair with the car. It's accepted wisdom that always comes up in discussions about mass transit, urban planning and budgets to fix potholes or build new highways. But a drive through the city's Automotive Historic District might convince you that it's true.

This unusual area near the city center was dedicated almost entirely to the car. Birmingham's first automobile dealership of any kind opened in 1904. (The White-Blakeslee Manufacturing Company sold gas and gasoline engines, pumping outfits, automobiles and supplies, according to the city directory. *Motor Age* magazine noted that Buick had given it the "agency" for the state of Alabama.) But as cars became more popular in the following years, the businesses that sold and serviced them began to cluster on the city's Southside, taking part in the redevelopment of a neighborhood that was transitioning from a mostly residential area to a commercial district.

Car dealerships, garages, repair shops and filling stations lined the blocks of the Automotive District, roughly defined by Twentieth Street South, First Avenue South, Twenty-fourth Street South and Fifth Avenue South. Some of the dealerships may have sold Premocars, the automobiles manufactured by the Birmingham-based Preston Motors Corporation at two plants in town. Many of these businesses also serviced motorcycles and the increasing numbers of delivery trucks on the city's streets.

The neighborhood today has shifted once again, and some of the old automobile-related spaces have been remodeled into offices, shops, restaurants and even a law school and entertainment venue. But a surprising number of car sales and repair companies remain in the area, keeping the Automotive Historic District, officially added to the National Register of Historic Places in 1991, alive and relevant to today's drivers.

REPUBLIC TIRES/UNITED AUTO SUPPLY

Tire shops helped to keep the Automotive District rolling. United Auto Supply opened at 421 Twentieth Street South in 1915, offering "everything to make driving pleasant and economical." (An old photograph even shows

a drive-up air pump right on the street and a young man on a motorcycle ready to deliver tires wherever needed.)

The business also sold Republic Tires. That company might have painted this sign as a privilege on the side of the United Auto Supply shop. Made by the Republic Rubber Company of Youngstown, Ohio, which incorporated in 1901, the tires featured "Staggard Tread," promoted in magazine ads as "the first effective rubber non-skid tire." Other ads highlight the "exclusive Prodium Process" rubber, which "ensures the slow, even wear of steel" and a "steel-like resistance to road-cuts and pavement-grinds." With all the talk of steel, Republic was in the right city.

Republic, which also made belts, hoses, valves, gaskets and a variety of other mechanical rubber goods in addition to tires, is now a brand owned by Goodyear. As for United Auto Supply, it moved a few blocks away from Twentieth Street by 1923 and seems to have expanded its services over the years. A 1952 ad promotes equipment for service stations and garages along with auto supplies. The company closed down by 1959.

United Auto Supply sold Republic Tires, a national brand, from a storefront at 421 Twentieth Street South between 1915 and the early 1920s. Faded words above the Republic name declare, "We have the prices and quality." The United Auto Supply name remains partially visible at the bottom of the ad, to the left of the newer paint. Jonathan Purvis.

BAMCO

While many car dealerships constructed new buildings in the neighborhood—even outfitting some with Italian marble tile, decorative terra-cotta façades and ramps to move cars between floors—existing buildings also were adapted for automotive uses. That was the case with the two-story structure on the corner of Second Avenue South and Twenty-fourth Street.

Constructed in about 1907, the building initially housed a saloon run by H.W. Eggler on the street level. The second floor was likely a rooming house or perhaps a business of a more lustful nature, considering that it was located on the edge of Birmingham's red-light district, which stretched along First Avenue South between Twenty-second and Twenty-fifth Streets early in the twentieth century. (The district was even officially sanctioned by the city between 1904 and 1913 as an attempt to confine the elements of "Bad Birmingham," as the city was known, to one area of town.)

Later, the building housed a soda bottling plant run by the Birmingham Fruit Beverage Company in 1920 and 1921 and the Birmingham Lime Cola Bottling Company in 1922. Lime Cola appears to have been a soft drink that originated in Montgomery in the 1910s and was bottled and sold throughout the South. One of these companies also manufactured Orange Crush and its sister drink, Lemon Crush. Directions for making the syrups for these drinks were discovered on a wall inside the building when it was renovated, and traces of a painted ad for Orange Crush, claiming that it is "made with luscious oranges," remain visible on the

This former saloon and soda bottling plant at Second Avenue South and Twenty-fourth Street became BAMCO (the Birmingham Auto and Machine Company) in 1931. Ads on the side and back walls listing available services and "any repair, any hour" may date from then or from 1919, when another garage operated there. *Jonathan Purvis.*

back wall. Later, a candy company took up residence.

Two firms adapted the building for auto-related businesses. A garage operated there in 1919, and the Birmingham Auto and Machine Company (BAMCO) took over in 1931, spelling out its name in letters across the front. Ads on the side and back walls of the structure list welding, tire straightening and ignitions among services offered and promise "any repair, any hour." It's not clear if these ads came from BAMCO, but if they did, all of that promotion didn't help George Farnsworth's company survive more than a year. By 1932, BAMCO was gone, and Perfection Laundry was using the building for its offices. The signs, along with the entire façade, were covered with stucco and ads for the mysterious-sounding Zoric Garment Cleaning System, a method of dry cleaning.

The BAMCO signs were uncovered when the building was adapted for yet another use in the 2000s. Today, the building houses an artist studio and renovation business.

GRAYSON ROSE TRANSMISSION COMPANY

"Friendly Grayson," the happy little cartoon character featured on the sign for the Grayson Rose Transmission Company, got his name—and his good nature—from the cofounder of the auto repair chain. According to Clyde Bolton, a former columnist for the *Birmingham News*, "Life was one big laugh to Rose. We were supposed to dance our way through it, having fun." He was a legendary practical joker, convincing good Samaritans to push a car with no engine along the highway, for example, or putting an opossum in his motel room and asking the desk clerk to remove the "mouse" from under the bed.

The infamous jester was also a famous local mechanic and car builder who was active in the early days of auto racing in Alabama. Stock car racing began with "whiskey trippers"—moonshine bootleggers—who relied on fast cars to outrun the police. The scofflaws would face off on rural dirt tracks to see whose car was fastest. Rose worked on cars for bootleggers, as well as the "revenuers" who chased them. He told Bolton, "As long as the whiskey trippers outran the feds, we all three had a job. Which one would you have made fastest?" Rose began working on stock cars as racing grew into a sport in the 1950s in places such as the Birmingham International Raceway at the Alabama state fairgrounds and on the beach in Daytona, Florida.

W. Cosby Hodges, a Birmingham businessman and an early auto racing record holder, founded the Grayson Rose Transmission Company in about 1958. Beginning with this location in a former auto paint shop and carpet cleaning facility at the edge of the Automotive District, the chain grew to include thirty-three franchised shops in eleven states. The company's advertising featured endorsements by racing icons Richard Petty and Bobby Allison, along with the claim that it was "the nation's largest rebuilders of pretested automatic transmissions." The trademark for Friendly Grayson was registered

Grayson Rose Transmission Service, named for a local mechanic who became a legend at the dawn of Alabama auto racing, opened at 2208 Sixth Avenue South in 1958. "Friendly Grayson," the cartoon mascot, came along by 1965, smiling at motorists—and potential customers—from ads on both sides of the building. The Grayson Rose company quickly grew into a franchise before it was purchased by an out-of-state company in 1968. *Jonathan Purvis.*

in 1965, indicating that this ad—along with another just like it on the other side of the building—was painted around that time.

In 1968, the Grayson Rose Transmission Company was purchased by the company now known as Mr. Transmission, and the new owners covered the exterior of this location in aluminum panels. The building later housed other auto-related businesses, and by 2010, it was ready for a renovation. The panels came down, revealing the ads along with a smaller painted placard identifying Grayson Rose's private parking space.

Rose himself died in 1973 and was posthumously inducted into the Alabama Racing Pioneers Hall of Fame. As for Friendly Grayson, he's welcoming a few new friends to his home. The former transmission shop has been remodeled and connected to an adjacent building to create Iron City Music Hall, a venue for bands and events.

SCHIMMEL HORSE SHOES

The switch from horse-drawn carriages and wagons to the automobile was not an instant one. When Birmingham's first car dealership opened in 1904, city directories listed ten livery, feed and sales stables; twenty-six blacksmiths; and four horseshoers. As modes of transportation changed, an entire industry centered on horses slowly began to vanish from the urban landscape; this made for an unusual mix of businesses in the growing Automotive District.

Some of the stables were converted into garages or warehouses, but other equine-

Look closely at the brick wall in the foreground, and "Horse Shoes" will begin to emerge. This ad on the side of 210 Twenty-second Street South pointed the way to Henry A. Schimmel's shop, which coexisted with cars in the growing Automotive District in the 1910s. The ad on the background building promotes Cream of Kentucky bourbon. *Jonathan Purvis.*

focused businesses, including blacksmiths and horseshoers, continued to serve their four-legged customers for years amid the roar of motorcar engines and the clangs emanating from auto shops. Henry A. Schimmel was among those holdout horseshoers, setting up shop—and painting his ad—along the stone-paved alley at 210 Twenty-second Street South in about 1914. He soon shared the block with two car dealerships, a seller of trucks, two auto repair shops, one tire repair business and the Clarence Auto Top Company.

Schimmel first appears in the Birmingham city directories in 1893, horseshoeing on Twentieth Street just south of the railroad tracks. In the early 1900s, he worked next to a livery stable at 208 Twenty-first Street South and then up the street in an alley next to the Wheelock building. Schimmel's directory ads from that time note that horses could be "called for and delivered" and that "interfering and faulty gaited horses receive special attention."

By the time Schimmel left Twenty-second Street in about 1919, the tide had definitely turned in favor of the horseless carriage; in fact, an auto garage became the next tenant of his space. Schimmel makes a final appearance in the city directories in 1922, horseshoeing on Eighteenth Street South.

Decades have passed since the *clip-clop* of hooves echoed through the alleys of the Automotive District, but several of the old stables and blacksmith shops remain standing, often unrecognizable in their current forms. Schimmel's former horseshoeing spot now has a garage door, and it is sandwiched between companies specializing in car alternators, starters and radiators.

Services

Birmingham was built on service. It was founded by a real estate company, after all, which catered to its customers by purchasing land, planning streets, selling property, establishing utilities and promoting the city as a good investment. And as soon as the first residents moved to the new town, entrepreneurs set up shop to meet the needs of both families and businesses. A letter written by one of the city's pioneers, Mrs. Alfred N. Hawkins (later published in John C. Henley's book *This Is Birmingham*), reports that a tinsmith, who both made and repaired metal goods, was one of the first enterprises to open.

Over time, Birmingham's service sector grew to rival its manufacturing base. The state's largest banks and financial firms made their home here. Lawyers and insurance companies populated downtown office towers. And the local newspapers filled with ads for companies eager to provide every service to make the reader's life and home happier, healthier, cleaner and prettier. In 1945, the University of Alabama's medical school moved to the Southside, marking the beginning of Birmingham's rise as a center for healthcare.

These service industries helped Birmingham to weather the economic blow when heavy industry declined in prominence toward the end of the twentieth century. Today, banks and biomedical research define the city just as much as furnaces and factories once did.

McCain Uniforms/Big Smith

Finding a friendly face in downtown Birmingham is easy. Just head to the corner of Third Avenue North and Twenty-second Street and look for the sharply dressed man. For nearly sixty years, he has smiled at passersby to promote McCain Uniforms, which called itself "the Uniform House of Dixie."

Founded in 1939, McCain outfitted workers in a variety of local industries—down to badges, holsters and rainwear. Printed ads promote custom-tailored clothes and dress suit rentals as additional services. The wall sign was likely painted in about 1956, when McCain moved into the building at 2208 Third Avenue North. A second ad on the wall shows the logo for Big Smith, a popular national brand of blue-collar workwear that originated in Missouri in 1916.

The Uniform House of Dixie
UNIFORMS
FOR EVERY PURPOSE
• BAND
• BOTTLERS
• BAKERIES
• BUS
• DAIRIES
• FIREMEN
• HOTEL
• MILITARY
• POSTMEN
• POLICE
LAW ENFORCEMENT EQPT.

Big Smith denim overalls were especially well known for their durability.

McCain also put its own name on the wall above the Big Smith ads, but eventually it was covered with white paint. Recently, the words have begun to reappear as the top coat fades.

The smiling man took up residence atop older generations of painted ads, and traces of them can still be seen on the wall. This building opened in about 1914 as the F.W. King and Company confectionery shop. Not long afterward, it housed a furniture company, but at some point in those early years, a large Coca-Cola ad was painted at ground level. Above it, toward the middle of the wall, was a sign for "Armature Winding." That term refers to the coils that wind around a motor and conduct an electrical current, creating a magnetic field. This sign may have directed customers to the Jeffrey Manufacturing Company, located next door in the 1940s. The Columbus, Ohio company made and sold construction equipment and mining machinery, including electric coal-cutting machines.

The wall also once hosted an ad for Vulcan Equipment and Supply Company, a wholesaler of hotel supplies, which occupied the former furniture store. In an old photograph, the sign lists Blakeslee kitchen appliances, dishes, glasses, potato peelers and ice crushers among merchandise for sale.

McCain left its friendly ambassador behind when it moved to another downtown location in 1987. Local historian Tim Hollis called it "perhaps Birmingham's most nostalgic sign" and a reminder of a time when American culture was more formal than it is today. "It really is a relic of a lost era," he said.

Opposite: McBride Sign Company painted this dapper gentleman for McCain Uniforms after "the Uniform House of Dixie" moved to 2208 Third Avenue North in about 1956. Weathering has revealed two or three layers of Coca-Cola ads below the McCain sign. The earliest of these may have been painted in about 1914, when the building was new. *Jonathan Purvis.*

Below: The ad for McCain Uniforms stretches the full length of the building. The section in the back, facing Twenty-second Street, features the logo for Big Smith matched uniforms and work clothing, a brand that McCain sold. "Armature Winding," barely visible above the billboard, may refer to a company that sold mining machinery on this block before McCain's arrival. *Jonathan Purvis.*

BERTHON'S CLEANERS

Growth and progress were dirty jobs in Birmingham's early decades, so it's no surprise that laundries and dry cleaners did a booming business in the days before most households owned washers and dryers.

Albert H. Berthon got a taste of the sooty city after immigrating to Jefferson County from France at age fourteen with his family. His first job was in a coal mine, but he soon traded that for stints as a baker and a barber for the steelworkers in the Pratt City neighborhood. The shoeshine boy at his barbershop also pressed pants, and the service became so popular that Berthon began to explore dry cleaning as a business.

At that time, dry cleaning consisted of scrubbing clothes with gasoline and then hanging them on a line to dry. Today, the lingering scent of gasoline is not something that most people would find appealing, but in the early 1920s, customers were eager to smell it. For them, it was proof that the clothes were clean.

Berthon soon quit barbering to focus solely on dry cleaning, and in 1925, he opened a new shop on Avenue E in Ensley. He had chosen Ensley, a former independent industrial town annexed into Birmingham in 1910, because its steel plants, blast furnaces and other factories had sparked a

Berthon's has operated dry cleaning stores in the Birmingham area, including the location at 2213 Avenue E in Ensley, since the 1920s. The colorful ad touting "Polarized Fur Care" and Berthon's "Blue Ribbon Service" first appeared sometime in the middle of the century. Since then, most likely in the 1980s, a group of painters named Maske, Turley and Don has restored it. *Jonathan Purvis.*

boom in both population and commercial development. A small fleet of Berthon's trucks crisscrossed the area to pick up and deliver laundry to customers' homes.

By the 1950s and 1960s, Berthon's offered "Blue Ribbon Service" from two locations and had a reputation for being able to clean anything, from furs and leather to drapes and wedding dresses. The Ensley store had been remodeled with a vault to store those furs during the warm months of the year—a popular service among dry cleaners. Berthon's was one of many shops in the region to use the "Polarized" fur care process, which surrounded furs with cold, circulating air and controlled humidity. One cleaner in another part of Alabama described the Polarized method in a newspaper ad as the best way to "deep clean, lusterize, and help prolong the life and beauty of your fur."

This ad featuring the Polarized polar bear, the Berthon's blue ribbon and a list of other services likely appeared on the wall of the flagship location in the 1950s or 1960s. The current ad, however, is a restoration of the original; an inscription at the bottom notes that it was fixed up by "Maske, Turley & Don." If Maske is the same painter who restored the Sentinel TV ad on Birmingham's Southside in the late 1980s, then it's a good assumption that the Berthon's sign was redone around the same time. As for Berthon's itself, the dry cleaning company is still in business, doing its best to keep Birmingham fresh and clean (and hopefully not smelling like gasoline).

REGAL-ANDRE

In 1884, the shaggy-haired citizens of Birmingham could get a trim at nine barbershops. Their choices included Frank McCree's Climax Shaving Parlors, which called itself the only first-class barbershop in the city and featured hot and cold baths, and Walker and Vassar, "Fashionable Barbers and Hairdressers," which presumably also sculpted the coifs of the city's women.

By 1931, the city had about 350 barbershops and beauty shops, specializing in finger waves, curls and other popular styles. A number of supply companies had also sprung up to service these businesses with the tools, shampoos, tonics, dyes and other necessities of the trade. That same year, the Andre Company opened its doors, followed by the Regal Company in 1932.

Competitors through the Great Depression and World War II, the two beauty supply companies had combined to form the Regal-Andre Company by 1944. The firm soon launched its beauty show, which brought hairdressers to Birmingham from across the South to learn new techniques and compete for prizes each year. One early winner was Ray Reed of Karr's Beauty Salon in Florence, Alabama, who used his wife, Tommie, as his model. The next year, the contest featured more than twenty-two contestants from six states. In 1952, the show, held at the Thomas Jefferson Hotel, was televised locally.

Regal-Andre opened in the building at 1711 Third Avenue North the year the companies merged, and the painted ads on the east and west walls likely date from around then. One of these ads covers two or three earlier signs that have

As the ad for Regal-Andre Company, painted after 1944 by United Sign Company, fades, older signs below it appear to sharpen. The ad at the roofline promotes Wallace and Allen Furniture Company, which opened at 1711 Third Avenue North in 1912. The giant letter "C" may belong to the Cable-Shelby-Burton piano company, located here in the 1930s. Another ad, which appears to show a can and perhaps a rainbow, remains a mystery. A few more years of weathering might reveal more of it. *Jonathan Purvis.*

left their marks. While an ad for the Wallace and Allen Furniture Company, which occupied the premises from 1912 to about 1920, is barely visible, the other faded signs are even less legible. One seems to include the illustration of a can and perhaps a rainbow. This could be connected with the Republic Wall Paper and Paint Company, housed in the building in 1932. The letter "C" probably belonged to the Cable-Shelby-Burton Piano Company, which had a showroom in the space just a few years later.

Regal-Andre stayed at the Third Avenue address until about 1963, when the company relocated to Fourth Avenue South. The firm continued to meet the city's hairstyling needs until 1988.

Harris Transfer and Warehouse Company

The year 1880 was a good one for Birmingham—and for George C. Harris. The Alice Furnace blast furnaces had started production, and newly inaugurated factories such as the Birmingham Rolling Mills were drawing a steady stream of job seekers. Harris, a Blount County native, saw his own opportunity for prosperity in that influx of people, launching the Harris Transfer Company to help them move their belongings into and around the city.

The firm originally consisted of one employee (George himself), one horse and one wagon, but it quickly grew along with the city. An 1888 ad in a city directory noted that the Harris company could "transfer household goods, etc. on short notice." In 1912, the firm cranked up its first motorized moving van, though it continued to rely on draft horses and wagons for some jobs until the 1940s. The company also built warehouses for household goods and for the storage and distribution of merchandise. By 1937, Harris was one of the South's largest storage and transfer firms, with three warehouses and more than sixty motor vehicles.

The first of these warehouses rose in 1916 on the corner of Sixth Avenue South and Twenty-second Street, on the site of the company's horse stables in the middle of a residential neighborhood. (Obviously, zoning regulations didn't exist then.) The four-story building had doors wide enough for both horses and trucks. However, demand for storage quickly

Harris Transfer and Warehouse Company constructed a large building on the corner of Sixth Avenue South and Twenty-second Street in 1916 and then added a second warehouse next door about seven years later to meet the growing demand for household storage. The signs may have appeared in the 1920s or 1930s, when Harris Transfer opened another warehouse near the railroad tracks. *Jonathan Purvis.*

outstripped the supply of space, and in about 1923, the Harris company built a larger, five-story warehouse next door.

Ads painted on every side of the two structures listed the Harris name and boasted of 150,000 square feet of storage space for household goods, specifically mentioning pianos, considered prized possessions at the time. Other signs on the roof of the new warehouse reassured customers that it was "Fire-Proof." It's unclear exactly when the ads appeared, but they were on the wall by some point in the 1930s, when the Harris company opened a warehouse for commercial merchandise near the railroad tracks. The first warehouse in its collection ended up with the "no. 3" designation.

Harris Transfer and Warehouse Company remained in business for more than a century and continued to use the two warehouses along Twenty-second Street until it went bankrupt in the 1990s. Today, the buildings contain self-storage units, except for the first floor, which was remodeled to house the popular Fish Market restaurant. The owners of the self-storage business saw some value in the old painted ads, restoring the words "Storage Warehouse" at the top of the building.

While George Harris's company may be gone, part of his legacy continues to roll on the streets of Birmingham and other cities around the country. In 1930, Harris Transfer joined with other major transfer companies to form Allied Van Lines, considered the first nationwide system for long-distance moving.

AMERICAN LIFE INSURANCE COMPANY

Birmingham is historically known for making tough, solid things such as iron and steel. But the city has been a longtime leader in more intangible industries such as insurance. Birmingham is the birthplace of a number of regional and national companies, including Liberty National and Protective Life, and today it continues to serve as the headquarters for several insurers.

Insurance has always been a profitable business in the city, it seems. The 1883–84 city directory lists nine insurance representatives, some of whom also acted as real estate agents or lawyers. (In comparison, there were thirteen restaurants and seven dry goods stores.) Just sixteen years later, more than one hundred entries for insurance companies clog the directory pages.

The American Life Insurance Company joined their ranks in 1931. Formed in a merger of two similarly named local firms—the American Security Life Insurance Company and the American Standard Life Insurance Company—the new business specialized in "ordinary and industrial insurance," according to one print ad. By 1947, the combined company had moved into the Martin Building, identifying its new headquarters by painting "American Life" atop the east and north sides of the twelve-story tower.

The Martin Building had an illustrious past. Opened in about 1925, it served as the temporary home for the city government after fire destroyed the Birmingham City Hall the same year. The Birmingham Division of the Federal Bureau of Investigation also occupied part of the building from 1947 to 1962, a period when civil rights–related violence grew in the city. Other tenants over the years included architects, advertising agencies, engineering companies, physicians and representatives of national manufacturing firms, from Hershey chocolate to Lorillard tobacco.

American Life's headquarters had moved to Texas by 1960, but it remained active in

The 1920s Martin Building on the corner of Fourth Avenue North and Twenty-third Street became the American Life Building in the 1940s, when the insurance company of the same name moved its headquarters there. A related firm, Stonewall Insurance Company, succeeded American Life in the tower in the 1960s and exited in 1979. *Jonathan Purvis.*

casualty and auto insurance, continued doing business there until 1979.

Through many purchases, acquisitions and mergers, the two insurance companies still exist. American became part of the American-Amicable Life Insurance Company of Waco, Texas, and Stonewall is now a Rhode Island company. In Birmingham, the Stonewall Building eventually served as a document storage center before becoming vacant in about 2000. For several years, developers planned to renovate the tower into condominiums or apartments. Economic conditions put that project on hold, as well as other proposals to use the building as offices, a hotel and an assisted living facility. Today, it sits empty, continuing to hold high its painted banner for American Life.

LAWYERS TITLE

Just thirty years after the city sprouted from a muddy cornfield, the first skyscrapers rose from Birmingham's streets. The ten-story Woodward Building led the way in 1902, closely followed the next year by the Title Building on the corner of Third Avenue North and Richard Arrington Jr. Boulevard. Both buildings were designed by the same architect, William C. Weston, and both cost about $300,000 to construct.

The Title Building was named for the company that built it, the Title Guaranty and Trust Company. But according to its early promoters, the edifice also held the title of the best-equipped, most complete office building in the South. Tenants received free electricity courtesy of an in-house power plant. They could also choose to get their water from the

Alabama. Within two years, it had gained control of the Stonewall Insurance Company, the state's oldest insurance firm, and relocated it to Birmingham from Mobile, where it had been founded nearly a century earlier. The company moved into the American Life Building, renaming it the Stonewall Building in about 1967. The Stonewall company, focusing on fire,

Lawyers Title
Insurance Corporation
Title Guarantee
DIVISION
ABSTRACTS
TITLE INSURANCE

city or from a groundwater reservoir below the building.

Title Guaranty would become the oldest title company in Alabama, specializing in abstracts, title insurance and trusts to protect people against risks related to property ownership in real estate transactions. By 1920—and perhaps much earlier—the company had painted black-and-white ads listing its name and services in large, bold letters on the north and west sides of the tower. The placement of these ads was important. Not only did they have high visibility because the building was the tallest for several blocks, but they also hovered over two key routes to the county courthouse, then located across the street from the Title Building. They were positioned perfectly to catch the eyes of potential customers.

The Title Guaranty ads were repainted several times with slight variations in wording, but the Third Avenue sign received its final form after 1961, when Title Guaranty became part of the Virginia-based Lawyers Title Insurance Corporation. Curiously, the existing painted sign is credited to Dixie Neon, the company responsible for some of Birmingham's most famous nighttime spectaculars, including the iconic red City Federal sign. While Dixie Neon did create some painted signs with neon overlays, no evidence shows that the Lawyers Title ad included anything more than paint.

Title Guaranty had painted black-and-white ads for its insurance services on the sides of its namesake building since the 1920s. The current ad dates from the period between 1961, when the company became a subsidiary of Lawyers Title Insurance Corporation, and 1976, when it relocated from the tower. Dixie Neon is responsible for this sign, even though no actual neon may have been involved. *Jonathan Purvis.*

Lawyers Title moved from the Title Building in about 1976, and a decade later, the tower was renovated to house a real estate firm and other tenants.

The northern sign was not repainted when Lawyers Title took ownership. By then, the street had become a one-way route, and drivers might see the ad only in their rear-view mirrors. Even today, the sign hides in plain sight above a steady stream of traffic.

FITZPATRICK BONDING COMPANY

The 1800 block of Third Avenue North in Bessemer may be the most law-abiding thoroughfare in Jefferson County. Nearly every building houses legal offices of some sort, including plenty of attorneys and bonding companies. What caused this clustering of justice? The root lies in a long-simmering rivalry between two boomtowns that nearly split Jefferson County in two.

Bessemer was founded in 1887 by Henry F. DeBardeleben, an iron and steel tycoon who wanted to build an industrial city from scratch. On a four-thousand-acre plot of land, he laid out a town along a railroad and built four blast furnaces in the area. The city, named for Sir Henry Bessemer, inventor of the open-hearth method of producing steel, became a population magnet. By the 1920s, Bessemer was Alabama's fourth-largest city, earning the nickname "the Marvel City" for its rapid growth.

Meanwhile, new residents continued to flood into the Magic City, making Birmingham one of the nation's fastest-growing cities in the

Fitzpatrick Bonding Company used its wall wisely, placing an ad for its day-or-night bail bonds service right outside the door to the Bessemer Courthouse. The company painted over one or more existing signs after it opened at 1813 Third Avenue North in 1960. An ad just above it gives accused scofflaws the name of a nearby attorney. *Jonathan Purvis.*

One plan carved a large chunk of western Jefferson County, along with portions of Bibb, Shelby, Tuscaloosa and Walker Counties, to create a new Bessemer County. Another simply apportioned part of Jefferson to a new county named Pettus, honoring an Alabama-born Confederate brigadier general who later served in the United States Senate.

Although both plans failed, the Alabama legislature passed a compromise proposal in 1915. The law called for a Bessemer division within Jefferson County and created a special tax to fund a second courthouse to handle legal affairs for the "Bessemer Cutoff." Legal firms filled the surrounding block after the courthouse was built on Third Avenue North in 1920.

Fitzpatrick Bonding Company opened on the 1800 block in 1960, offering bail bonds at any hour for people accused of crimes. It scored a prime location next door to the courthouse, and its painted sign would have been a welcome sight to suspected lawbreakers entering and exiting the halls of justice. A smaller ad promotes an attorney by the name of Bains, another potential source of legal assistance. Both signs were painted over at least one earlier ad; the words "List Property for Sale" are faintly visible.

The rivalry between Bessemer and Birmingham has subsided, but justice never rests. Today, the Bessemer Courthouse remains a satellite of the Jefferson County government, and Fitzpatrick continues to issue bonds from the lawyer-lined street.

first decade of the twentieth century. Some residents of Bessemer and surrounding areas didn't like Birmingham's dominance over the rest of Jefferson County, however. Beginning in the 1890s, their elected officials made proposal after proposal to create a new county with Bessemer as its seat.

Entertainment

Building Birmingham into an industrial powerhouse was no easy job. So when the workweek ended, its citizens were ready to play, laugh, dance and be dazzled as hard as they had worked.

In the early years, audiences could choose from a variety of stage spectacles. Revues, burlesque and minstrel shows were popular, as was vaudeville, which featured everything from musicians, dancers and comedians to magicians, ventriloquists and trained animals. Melodramas also thrilled audiences with tales of romantic heroes fighting wily villains to rescue damsels in distress.

Performing arts that were gaining in popularity around the country also found a home in the young city. The Birmingham Historical Society wrote that the "legitimate stage achieved an all-time high level of activity" in the first decades of the twentieth century, producing "the dress styles, the dance steps, the jokes and slang that made up the American scene." Birmingham's theaters offered elegant evenings out, with operas and dramas starring nationally known actors and actresses.

The first local movie theater opened in 1905, and competitors soon popped up to cash in on the moving-picture craze. (In 1977, the Birmingham Historical Society reported that seventy-three different movie theaters had served downtown over the decades.) Many of the original theaters were housed in small retail spaces that had been outfitted with nothing more than seats, a projector and a sheet for a screen. But as the movies got bigger, so did the movie houses, culminating in lavish movie palaces such as the Ritz and the Alabama.

Theaters weren't the only game in town, however. Bowling alleys, billiard parlors and dance halls were all popular. A collection of African American music venues, located where two streetcar lines crossed in Ensley, became the inspiration for "Tuxedo Junction," a classic jazz tune co-written by Birmingham native Erskine Hawkins and made popular by Glenn Miller and His Orchestra.

The arrival of television—and then computers and digital media—greatly expanded the availability of entertainment, though the experience was more personal than communal. In the past few decades, however, fun-seekers have come back to the city to see movies and concerts at the restored Alabama and Carver Theatres, to enjoy plays and musicals in a variety of venues and to attend art, film and music festivals right on the streets. The fading ads representing each era of entertainment prove that the show does indeed go on and that there's always a new star waiting in the wings.

LYRIC THEATRE

In 2010, the fading sign on the side of downtown's Lyric Theatre got its first fresh coat of paint in at least eighty years. This time, however, the goal of the ad was not to promote the Favorite Players, a repertory company that performed at the Lyric in the 1920s. Instead, the sign is helping to raise public awareness of the theater itself and the ongoing project to restore the Lyric as a fine arts venue.

A night at the Lyric was a hot ticket when the theater debuted in 1914 as part of the B.F. Keith Vaudeville circuit. (The earliest version of the Lyric's painted ad includes Keith's name rather than the Favorite Players.) National stars, including the Marx Brothers, Mae West, Will Rogers, Milton Berle and Jack Benny, walked its stage. Cartoonist Rube Goldberg performed on opening night. Audiences paid twenty-five to seventy-five cents for a seat in the ornate auditorium, which was specifically designed for vaudeville with acoustics that amplify live performances and steep balconies and box seats that give everyone a close view of the stage.

Here, as elsewhere in Birmingham, segregation laws were enforced. African American customers entered the theater through a separate doorway around the corner from the main entrance. Once inside, they had to climb to the top of the highest balcony to find their seats. Surprisingly, that was a mark of progress in 1914. African Americans and whites could watch the same performance at the same time, and they would pay the same price to do it—a novel concept in the South.

The Lyric became the king of vaudeville in Birmingham when it opened on the corner of Third Avenue North and Eighteenth Street, in the middle of the district that local historians call "Birmingham's Broadway." Its success added to the city's thriving live performance scene, with the Bijou/Pantages, the Majestic, the Temple, the Ritz and smaller venues such as the Amuse-U and the Vaudette lighting up the nights. Most were part of chains such as Lowe's or Pantages, which sent performers on tours of their stages around the country. Birmingham also had the Jefferson Theatre, which presented elaborate traveling stage shows such as *Ben-Hur* and *Peter Pan*. Its own resident troupe eventually moved to the Lyric, performing light comedy as the Favorite Players from 1927 to 1930.

Vaudeville performances were, in essence, variety shows. Each one featured dozens of acts ranging from piano players and other musicians to magicians, contortionists, child prodigies, animal acts, jugglers and more. Comedians often won top billing and the most fame. Everyone found something to enjoy, and the mix won over a broad range of audiences. A piece written for PBS's American Masters website describes vaudeville as "the earliest entertainment to cross racial and class boundaries" and "symbolic of the cultural diversity of early 20th-century America." For many watching the shows, the article continues, "vaudeville was the first exposure to the cultures of people living right down the street."

The original version of the Lyric Theatre's ad promoted the B.F. Keith vaudeville circuit and likely premiered along with the venue when it opened at the corner of Third Avenue North and Eighteenth Street in 1914. The Famous Players came along in 1927, staging productions for three years. Recently, the fading ad received a meticulous restoration as a step toward the renovation of the Lyric as a fine arts theater. *Jonathan Purvis.*

The rise of radio and the movies offered entertaining alternatives to vaudeville and hastened its decline. In Birmingham, the Great Depression added to the blow, forcing the Lyric to close as a vaudeville theater by 1931. From 1932 until about 1960, the Lyric showed movies, and it briefly flickered to life again in the 1970s to present classic films. Within a few years, the grand vaudeville palace was home to the Foxy and Roxy adult cinemas.

Another kind of movie came to the Lyric in 1976—and this time, the theater and its fading ad appeared onscreen. That year, Birmingham served as the shooting location for *Stay Hungry*, a story of love and bodybuilding starring Jeff Bridges, Sally Field and Arnold Schwarzenegger

in one of his first big roles. In an unforgettable scene, near-naked contestants from the Mr. Universe competition run through the downtown streets and strike poses on the Lyric's fire escapes, perfectly framing the fading ad.

Alabama Landmarks, the organization that refurbished the Alabama Theatre across the

street, took ownership of the Lyric in 1993
and has developed plans and a fundraising
campaign for its restoration. The goal calls for
the transformation of the Lyric into a 1,200-
seat venue for live music, dance and drama
to complement the Alabama and nearby
Carver Theatre. The six-story office building
surrounding the Lyric would also be renovated,
possibly as a home for arts organizations.

LUCKY STRIKE BOWLING ALLEYS

The reappearance of this ad certainly is a lucky
strike. In 2010, an unknown person pried a
concrete panel off the façade of the vacant
American Red Cross building. No one knows
why the culprit did it. No doubt he or she got
quite a surprise upon discovering the seventy-
year-old ad—an item with historical value
rather than monetary value.

The Lucky Strike Bowling Alleys opened
in 1941 in a converted furniture store on the
bottom floor of a building housing fraternal
organizations. Next door was the former
Municipal Market, which had been recycled
into a garage for auto repairs and car rentals.
Curiously, the sign for Lucky Strike seems to have
been painted on a wall of the garage and not on
the building housing the alleys. Perhaps the two
businesses were connected; a print ad from 1944
notes that Lucky Strike also rented cars.

Bowling was a big deal just before World
War II. A *Birmingham News* article counted half
a dozen alleys in the downtown area alone.
Many, like Lucky Strike, made their homes
in empty retail spaces; a few opened in the
basements of buildings.

Lucky Strike Bowling Alleys, which operated at 2217
Third Avenue North in downtown Birmingham from
1941 to 1948, had been forgotten until a vandal
unearthed this ad in 2010. The sign survived because
it was painted on the building next door to the alleys
and then concealed under concrete panels added in a
renovation. The alley building was demolished in about
1957. *Jonathan Purvis.*

Lucky Strike lasted just seven years. Before it closed, the garage building had been remodeled and expanded into an office building for the Birmingham branch of the Social Security Administration and other federal offices. The bowling alleys' painted sign was hidden behind one of the concrete panels used to reface the building.

The Birmingham chapter of the American Red Cross later occupied the building, and the former home of Lucky Strike was torn down to create a parking lot. Everyone forgot about the heyday of bowling in downtown Birmingham until a curious vandal came along.

SENTINEL TELEVISIONS

The age of television arrived in Birmingham on June 12, 1949, when WAFM took to the airwaves. The city's first TV channel was a branch of local radio station WAPI, and it wasn't long—less than a month, in fact—before a competing radio station, WBRC, began airing its own TV programs.

TV back then was quite different than it is today. For example, until Birmingham was connected to coaxial cables in 1950, the city couldn't see any live network broadcasts. Programmers also had to divide shows from the Big Four networks at the time—NBC, CBS, ABC and DuMont—between the city's two stations. Nevertheless, TV became enormously popular, and sets were big sellers. By the 1950s, Wimberly-Thomas Hardware, a decades-old wholesaler of agricultural implements and mill and mine supplies, was stocking sporting goods and appliances—possibly including televisions.

The Sentinel TV ad appeared on the wall of the Wimberly-Thomas warehouse on

The ad for the "Picture-Sealed" Sentinel TV has become a colorful landmark at 1801 First Avenue South near Railroad Park. Originally painted during the 1950s, it was restored by painters Maske and Reese about thirty years later. In 2012, the building owners stated their intent to preserve the ad after it faced the threat of removal. *Jonathan Purvis.*

First Avenue South in about 1953. A print ad from that year depicts the same scene, with an elegantly dressed trio (and a large plant) enthralled by a woman on the tube. Promotional copy claims that the "Picture-Sealed TV" offers "clear, big pictures without 'flip, flap, or flutter,'" as well as perfect reception in both the city and country. Prices started at $199.95.

"The Picture Stayed" could describe this wall sign as well as Sentinel TVs, because it has survived two brushes with oblivion. A black-and-white photograph from 1961 shows that it had been painted over, with faint shapes on the wall matching the placement of the people in the ad. By 1969, a newly constructed building blocked the space where the mural hung. The Sentinel ad likely was repainted in the 1980s, when the Wimberly-Thomas warehouse was renovated into the Midtown Center office complex and the building on the side was removed. The ad itself credits "Maske and Reese" with the ad's restoration; unfortunately, these painters left few traces, so we don't know who they were. (Maske's name also appears on the restored Berthon's Cleaners sign in Ensley.)

In 2012, the owners of the Midtown Center won a reluctant approval from the Birmingham Design Review Committee to paint over the mural as part of an effort to repair and reseal the wall. A public outcry to save the sign immediately followed, and the owners changed their plans, claiming that they had found another method of fixing the wall that would protect the ad. Fans of the Sentinel sign are staying tuned to see what happens.

COLOR TV

This vibrant sign premiered in 1966, the year that the three major television networks—ABC, CBS and NBC—began airing all of their prime-time programming in color. Viewers could finally see the green of *Green Acres*, along with the true hues of *Bonanza*, *Bewitched*, *Lawrence Welk*, *Andy Griffith*, *Ed Sullivan* and *The Beverly Hillbillies*.

That was a turning point in the development of color television. Though color broadcasts had hit the airwaves more than a decade before, consumers were slow to buy color TV sets, which cost between $1,000 and $1,295 in 1954—about the same price as a car. It wasn't until the networks began broadcasting mostly in color, led by NBC in 1965, that audiences began to switch to the new format in large numbers.

TV dealers responded to the increased demand by stocking models such as Magnavox (with Magna-Color, Astro-Sonic stereo and a new innovation called the remote control), Zenith, RCA Victor, Motorola, Sylvania, Philco, General Electric and Admiral. In the Edgewood neighborhood of Homewood, Henderson Floyd and Don Addington opened TV Sales and Service in the business district on Oxmoor Road, painting this ad on their side wall to announce their arrival.

The shop lasted only a year, however, and a billboard was eventually constructed over the ad. In the meantime, the sales of color TV sets grew, overtaking the sales of black-and-white sets in 1972. But the billboard ended up protecting Floyd and Addington's ad from the sun's color-zapping rays. When the sign came down in the 2000s, the painted ad was

Concealed behind a billboard for a few decades, the ad for TV Sales and Service retains much of its original vibrant color from 1966. Owned by Henderson Floyd and Don Addington, the shop at 1003 Oxmoor Road in Homewood sold a variety of models, including sets that offered both color and black-and-white viewing. *Jonathan Purvis.*

so bright and crisp that it could have been advertising a new product. Today, its brightness has begun to fade in the light, but it retains the feel of a color TV time capsule in an HDTV world.

STARR PIANO COMPANY

When the Starr Piano Company's shadow of a sign was freshly painted, the street below rang with melody. Four piano stores dueled for customers in the space of two blocks; later, they were joined by music teachers and an emporium of instruments, sheet music, records, radios and phonographs. When windows were open on a warm day, the street must have sounded like the backstage area of a concert hall before a big performance.

Starr struck the first note when it moved into the building at 1820 Third Avenue North in about 1913. At that time, the piano was the primary medium for distributing popular music—a role later occupied by records, radio, cassettes, CDs and mp3s. Families would gather around their pianos to perform tunes purchased as sheet music. The instruments quickly evolved into symbols of status and culture, and the piano became a central fixture in the home.

A merger of two piano manufacturers in 1893 created Starr, and the Richmond, Indiana firm became known for the quality of its instruments. Soon the company had stores in cities nationwide, including Birmingham. As music technology and tastes changed, Starr

began making player pianos, piano rolls and, in 1915, phonographs and records.

Under its Gennett label, Starr "would record practically any musician, regardless of race, who might produce a profitable record," notes a history on the Starr-Gennett Foundation website. The company was a pioneer in recording jazz and blues, issuing some of the first records by future legends Jelly Roll Morton, Louis Armstrong, Duke Ellington and Hoagy Carmichael. Later, Gennett released early country records, including songs by Gene Autry. The success of these records proved that there was a demand for these types of music and inspired other labels to follow suit. Other Gennett records spotlighted regional and ethnic sounds, including Native American tribal songs, Hawaiian guitar and midwestern dance bands.

Some of the southern blues, jazz and gospel acts were recorded in this building, in a temporary studio set up on the third floor in 1927. Starr relied on location recording to identify new talent far from its permanent studios in New York and Indiana, venturing to places such as Chicago, Cincinnati, Minneapolis–St. Paul and the Grand Canyon. The Birmingham studio, open for only three months, was the company's only southern stop. "The nation looks to the South for its Dixie melodies, its jazz orchestras, its hot music," said Starr sound

engineer Gordon Soule to the *Birmingham News* in July 1927.

Local and regional music-makers flocked to the Starr studio on Third Avenue. There, William Harris became one of the first Mississippi Delta blues guitarists to make a record, and Jaybird Coleman, a blues harmonica player from Alabama, performed a song with the evocative title "Ah'm Sick and Tired of Tellin' You (To Wiggle That Thing)." Other blues, jazz, and gospel acts recording in Birmingham included the Black Birds of Paradise, the Triangle Harmony Boys, Frank Bunch and His Fuzzy Wuzzies and Syd Valentine's Patent Leather Kids.

In August 1927, a group of men and women known as J. T. Allison's Sacred Harp Singers made some of the first recordings of that particular style of southern religious folk music, sung a capella from a book that uses four "shape-notes" to help singers identify sounds on the musical scale. Members of the group included a railroad inspector and church music leader, a pipe foundry worker and a carpenter and clock repairman. After their two Birmingham recordings sold well, the Allison singers traveled to the Gennett studios in Richmond, Indiana, where they recorded thirty songs in one day.

The music began to fade soon afterward, as the Great Depression took hold. Slower sales led Gennett to stop producing records in 1930, two years before the Starr piano showroom in Birmingham moved from this building to another location. Starr, which had added refrigerators to its product line in the 1930s, made pianos until 1949. A branch of the company remains in business today under the name Refrigeration Supplies Distributor.

The Starr Piano Company operated a showroom in the building at 1820 Third Avenue North from about 1913 to 1932. An upstairs recording studio helped to introduce Alabama blues, jazz and gospel singers to a national audience in the 1920s. *Jonathan Purvis.*

RAINBOW'S END

In 1981, entertainment options were in short supply in the neighborhood of Avondale, just east of downtown Birmingham. The community had been battered by the closure of the large Avondale Mills textile factory a decade earlier, as well as the movement of residents and businesses from the inner city to the suburbs.

Parkway Christian Fellowship, a church in Huffman, another eastern neighborhood, attempted to liven things up by establishing its youth program on Avondale's main street. It set up shop as the Rainbow's End on the first floor of a fraternal lodge built in 1902 for the International Order of Odd Fellows, an organization dedicated to charitable causes. According to Marc Bondarenko, who later bought the building to serve as a photography studio, the Rainbow's End was a mixture of hangout space and arcade, capitalizing on the video game craze of the early 1980s.

The Rainbow's End soon met its own end, lasting only a year. Thirty years later, the neighborhood surrounding the former arcade has changed. Avondale is developing into an entertainment destination, with a brewery, restaurants, art galleries and music venues opening in recent years, anchored by a multimillion-dollar renovation of Avondale Park down the street. Visitors won't find a pot of gold near the rainbow sign, but they will discover new opportunities to enjoy themselves.

The Rainbow's End opened in 1981 as an Avondale activity center sponsored by a church youth program. Located at 212 Forty-first Street South, the space closed just a year later. *Jonathan Purvis.*

Places to Stay

If you were a new arrival to Birmingham in its earliest days, you didn't have much choice when it came to a place to rest your head. Soon after Birmingham was chartered in 1871, the Elyton Land Company built a two-story, wood-frame hotel alongside the railroad tracks to serve visitors to the new town. The thirty-seven-room Relay House was basic—with mosquito nets over each bed—but its wide porches and dining hall made it a destination for both travelers and local residents. The hotel was the setting for many of the city's social events and business meetings and served as a de facto train station as well.

As the city grew bigger and more sophisticated, so did its hotels. The ornate Morris, constructed in the 1890s, featured an arcade roof with glass that shed light on a colored-tile floor. Diners in its restaurant, lined with walls of mahogany and oak, drank out of crystal hand-engraved with the hotel's emblem. Just a few years earlier, the gilded dome of the Caldwell Hotel towered over First Avenue; underneath, guests enjoyed a sumptuous lobby with hand-carved furniture and dined in the light of a chandelier hanging two stories above their heads. The most elegant of Birmingham accommodations, however, may have been the original Tutwiler Hotel, which opened on Twentieth Street in 1914 with more than three hundred rooms, a grand lobby, marble walls, ornate décor and a glass-roofed courtyard.

Other, more basic options catered to travelers of modest means and African Americans barred from staying at the city's finest establishments. In the 1960s, the A.G. Gaston Motel on Fifth Avenue North became Birmingham's most famous place to stay. Originally built as premier accommodations for African American visitors, the motel hosted Martin Luther King Jr. and other civil rights leaders as they orchestrated the 1963 Birmingham campaign; it was bombed the same year.

While most of the city's classic downtown hotels have closed, been demolished or, as in the Tutwiler's case, reopened in a new building, their legacy of hospitality remains embedded in Birmingham's history.

THOMAS JEFFERSON HOTEL

The Roaring Twenties had a last hurrah in Birmingham with the debut of the nineteen-story Thomas Jefferson Hotel, located on the corner of Seventeenth Street and Second Avenue North. The lavish opening celebration on September 17, 1929, just weeks before the Wall Street crash, featured a dinner, dancing and a "gay cabaret party" starring the Keep Smiling Revue, the Kit Kat Trio and an orchestra playing "snappy jazz" under a full moon. According to a report in the *Birmingham Post*, four hundred attendees partied for hours on an outdoor terrace, showered from above with confetti and balloons. And they went home in the wee hours of the morning with souvenirs, including caps "that made one resemble a French artist, a clown, or what not, clappers, horns, balloons, compacts for the girls, razor sets for the men, boxes of nuts that turned out to be rubber, souvenir packets containing one's fortune" and even tiny bells to wear around their ankles.

Designed by local architect D.O. Whilldin for $2.5 million and operated by the Texas-based Baker Corporation, the hotel was opulent by any city's standards. The *Post* noted that the 350 rooms included suites furnished in early American, colonial or modernistic styles, and each had running ice water. In a nod to prohibition, a corkscrew and bottle opener—"naturally, for the use of mineral water bottles," noted the newspaper—were attached to the wall in each bathroom. A banquet hall, lounge, coffee shop and private dining rooms made up the public areas downstairs, and atop

the tower stood a mooring mast for dirigibles, built in anticipation of future passenger service to Birmingham. Another unusual amenity was an insurance policy that covered each guest against accidental death, injury and disability for twenty-four hours after checkout. By 1936, rates started at $2.50 a night.

Two white-on-black painted ads—a vertical one stretching ten and a half stories on the tower's west façade and a smaller horizontal version on the south side—identified the hotel from several blocks in both directions. In the 1950s, Dixie Neon maintained these signs and outlined the painted letters with neon tubes for nighttime illumination.

As one of Birmingham's largest and finest hotels, the Thomas Jefferson accommodated many celebrities over the years, from former presidents Calvin Coolidge and Herbert Hoover to entertainers George Burns, Ethel Merman, Mickey Rooney and Ray Charles. Legendary University of Alabama football coach Paul "Bear" Bryant had a top-floor suite in the 1970s. Many salesmen used the hotel as both home and office, reserving a second room to display their wares to customers.

By then, the Thomas Jefferson was facing serious challenges. Its location on the west side of downtown kept it isolated from the

The ten-and-a-half-story ad on the back of the Thomas Jefferson Hotel may have appeared once the building opened in 1929, but the existing version is credited to Dixie Neon, which lit up the letters at night. The tops of Birmingham's other towers sported painted ads for banks and even soft drinks over the years. *Jonathan Purvis.*

main business district and the other big hotels. Despite renovations in the 1960s and a 1972 name change to the Cabana Hotel—spelled out on the roof in neon, with a giant "C" hung on the mooring mast—the hotel continued to struggle. By the early 1980s, about two hundred residents, mostly elderly people, were paying $200 a month to live in the Cabana's rooms. The Jefferson County Health Department closed the building in 1983 over safety and health violations.

The building has been empty ever since, though California developer David Leer made plans for a $23 million renovation in 2005 that would have filled the old hotel with sixty high-end condominiums and added a rooftop pool. He even replaced the old Cabana signs with new ones reading "Leer Tower," the name for the project. Legal issues and the economic downturn of the late 2000s doomed the renovation, and today the building sits in disrepair, though local newspapers report that potential buyers are interested in turning the Jazz Age monument into apartments.

DENECHAUD HOUSE

In 1887, the new Denechaud European Hotel and Restaurant brought an elegant, foreign flair to the boomtown of Birmingham. E.F. Denechaud, the French-born proprietor, had operated a restaurant and lodging in New Orleans since the middle of the century. Seeing an opportunity in the growing city, he attempted to replicate his success in Alabama by putting two of his sons in charge. Edward A. Denechaud served as manager, while his brother Louis A. Denechaud was the hotel clerk. The establishment was one of eleven hotels and thirty restaurants in the city when it opened.

The hotel's name may indicate that it offered guests a European plan—a room only, with no meals covered by the rate—rather than the more inclusive American plan. Advertisements for the Denechaud restaurant and hotel in New Orleans from 1875 offer hints of the amenities that might have been offered in Birmingham, including "every delicacy of the market" and "the choicest imported wines, ales, etc., at very reasonable prices. Boarders by the week or month with or without lodging. Large and airy rooms, for private and Society Dinners. Special attention given to Supper and Wedding Parties at residence."

Alabama's Denechaud House lasted just two years. Louis returned to New Orleans and continued working as a clerk in his father's Hotel Denechaud. Under the management of another brother, Justin A. Denechaud, the hotel grew into one of the grandest and most luxurious accommodations in the South. Its building stands today as the Le Pavillon hotel.

Coincidentally, another famous New Orleans establishment has its roots in Birmingham, just around the corner from the Denechaud House. Jean Galatoire and his wife moved to Birmingham from France in 1874, opening a hotel and restaurant at 108 Twenty-first Street North. The family moved to Chicago in 1893, and at the turn of the century, they settled in New Orleans, where they opened their world-famous restaurant.

Over the years, the former Denechaud hotel and restaurant has housed a sewing machine company, a printing shop, a paint company,

Entrepreneurs from New Orleans operated the Denechaud European Hotel and Restaurant at 2107 Second Avenue North from 1887 to 1889. The sign was restored during a 1980s renovation of the building. *Jonathan Purvis.*

apartments, a furniture store, an architecture firm and a law office. When it came time to renovate the building in 1985–86, historic photos helped the architect reconstruct the original façade. Sign painters also restored the "Denechaud House" sign, which had been hidden behind a three-story building for many years.

FURNISHED ROOMS

People intending to stay longer than a few nights in the city—or who were making a permanent move—often boarded with local families or rented furnished rooms. Apartment buildings did not exist in Birmingham until the first years of the twentieth century.

Fortunately, most multistory buildings constructed in Birmingham's early years were designed to serve a dual purpose, with retail on the ground floor and residential space above. A prime example is the structure at 112–114 Twenty-fourth Street North, which has an ad for furnished rooms still visible next to the door leading upstairs to 112½. According to city directories, Mrs. C.B. Turner offered furnished rooms for rent here in 1902, followed by J.T. Allison in 1912 and J.S. Walker from 1922 through 1926. In a photo from 1940, the painted sign is not visible, but a projecting sign advertises rooms.

A building survey from the same year lists twelve rooms and one bathroom on the second floor. The rooms were likely rented out individually, though city directories for some years list only one occupant. Early volumes indicate that the second floor was once divided into two apartments.

No matter the arrangement, residents rarely stayed long, with tenants changing from year to year. The list of lodgers includes a dressmaker, a grocer, a saloonkeeper, a contractor, an auto mechanic and widow, among others. The most colorful resident may have been Madam Emma Mullen, who ran a brothel in the building in 1897.

Early residents also were connected with the retail establishments downstairs. The building appears on an 1885 map and is recorded in the 1889 city directory as an African American saloon run by L.O. Delamar and J.H. Robinson. Later first-floor occupants included grocery stores, a cigar shop, a fish seller and an auto repair business—all potentially fragrant neighbors for the tenants upstairs.

The last lodger moved out in the 1940s, and the building later housed an ironworkers' union and the Bomb Shelter, a rehearsal space and music venue, with artist studios on the second floor. Today, the building is empty, but the downtown district surrounding it has rediscovered the "mixed-use" concept, echoing the past by stacking residences above retail and office spaces. This time around, fortunately, there are no fish sellers among them.

Hundreds of people called the building at 112–114 Twenty-fourth Street North home over the years. The second floor offered furnished rooms in 1902, 1912, the 1920s and perhaps even later. *Jonathan Purvis.*

Beverages

Long before soft drinks got a bad rap for their sugar and other ingredients, they were considered health tonics. Several of America's most familiar sodas—Coca-Cola, Pepsi-Cola and Dr. Pepper, among others—originated during the 1880s and 1890s in drugstores, where pharmacists concocted formulas to ease a variety of ills. In a way, soft drinks resembled patent medicines, except they could be combined with carbonated water and sold by the glass at soda fountains.

The popularity of soft drinks boomed after soda manufacturers began bottling their products in the 1890s. Suddenly, people could consume sodas anywhere—they weren't limited to the fountains. In addition, soft drink syrup could be shipped by rail to bottling plants anywhere in the country, opening up the national market for beverages previously confined to a city or region.

Naturally, Coca-Cola, invented by Atlanta pharmacist John Pemberton in 1886, helped to lead the way in both bottling and branding, and its rapid growth inspired a host of competitors. Soft drink makers in every city were eager to develop the next Coca-Cola—or simply to copy the real thing.

Soda bottlers in Birmingham had two key allies in their quest to quench the city's thirst: Alabama's hot, humid climate and the prohibition of alcohol. In an essay on Birmingham's wild and wooly early days, Patricia McCarl wrote that "purity reform and temperance movements" in the city gained momentum after 1900. Their efforts led to an election in 1907 that turned Jefferson County dry the following year, which meant that Birmingham's numerous saloons faced the choice of selling soft drinks or closing. Though Jefferson County resumed alcohol sales just three years later, national prohibition came along in 1920 and lasted until 1933.

While the bans may have helped to cement Birmingham's attraction to soft drinks, they did little to dim the demand for alcohol. Breweries and distillers have made their home in the city since 1885, and recent changes in state law have launched a new generation of small breweries that are adding to the local tradition of liquid refreshment.

Wiseola

According to soft drink historian Dennis Smith, Birmingham consumed more Coca-Cola than anywhere else on earth in 1913, but its citizens also were quenching their thirst with a flood of homegrown sodas, with colorful names such as Gleeola, Cola-Nip, Dope, Nifty Cola, Celery Cola, Ozo-Olo and Rye-Ola. In fact, Smith reported, no city in America produced more brands of soft drinks than Birmingham before 1920.

Few traces remain from Birmingham's reign as king of colas, but Jimmy and Sue Johnson accidentally discovered one in their bathroom one night in 2010. They had been pulling plaster off an interior wall of the Hunter Furniture building, which they were renovating into a dog day care and a loft for themselves. In the second-floor area slated to become their bathroom, they removed the last layer of plaster and found feet—painted bird feet, to be exact. The surprised couple spent the next few hours ripping off the rest of the plaster to solve the mystery, uncovering this ad for Wiseola, a soft drink produced in Birmingham between 1905 and 1915.

Wiseola actually originated in 1903 as Nervola, a soda probably formulated by local beverage chemist Jefferson J. Peek. Smith wrote that when the federal government denied Nervola's trademark because a Pennsylvania soft drink carried a similar name, the Birmingham

Above: The Wiseola owl now watches over the Johnsons' bathroom. Architects complemented the old soft drink ad with a unique light fixture made from Coca-Cola bottles. *Jonathan Purvis.*

Opposite: An ad for Wiseola resurfaced after Jimmy and Sue Johnson pulled the plaster off the wall in their future loft. Painted before 1909, the sign for the Birmingham-made soft drink spent a century hidden in the wall of the Hunter Furniture store at 112 Eighteenth Street North. *Amy P Photography, amypphotography.com.*

soda was rechristened Wiseola, and its owl trademark was born.

The public was encouraged to "get wise" to the drink, and they made it a popular choice at soda fountains and in bottles. Plants in Georgia and North Carolina helped to bottle and distribute Wiseola regionally. But the company faced a challenge in 1910 when the United States government took Wiseola and other soft drink manufacturers across the country (including Coca-Cola) to court, claiming violations of the Pure Food and Drug Act.

Passed four years earlier, the law took aim at "adulterated or misbranded or poisonous or deleterious foods, drugs, medicines, and liquors." Wiseola was found to contain traces of cocaine, but that wasn't the illegal part, according to the way the judgment reads; instead, the government cracked down on Wiseola because its labels did not list the drug as an ingredient. The company received the maximum fine—twenty-five dollars—and shut down its bottling operations in Birmingham for a few years, but it continued to produce syrup for bottling elsewhere. The Wiseola company reorganized in 1912 but was out of business for good within three years.

The Johnsons' Wiseola ad was painted before 1909, the year that their building—or another two-story structure—appears at 112 Eighteenth Street North in the city directories. Previously, the Wiseola ad hung on the outside wall of an adjacent building that was in use by 1899 and housed a variety of businesses over the years. (Other painted ads discovered on the Wiseola wall identify two neighbors: Linnehan Furniture Company, active from 1900 to 1903, and the Birmingham Pressing Club, a laundry cleaning service that occupied a space in 1906. Henry

Uhl, a sign painter located next door at the time, may have created some of these ads.)

The Johnsons' building had a variety of tenants itself, including a shoe repair shop and a saloon, before the Hunter family moved its furniture store there in the 1920s. They remained at the location for more than eight decades before closing the business in 2009. The building next door was torn down for parking in the mid-1980s, leaving behind only its shared wall.

After the Johnsons discovered the Wiseola ad in their future home, they worked with their architects to reorient their plans for the bathroom, enabling the painting to stay intact. The architects also sealed the ad to preserve it, and in a nod to the soda's history, they created a unique light fixture out of glass Coca-Cola bottles to softly illuminate the Wiseola owl.

GRAPICO

Two of Birmingham's homegrown beverages have survived long beyond the high-water mark of regional soft drinks. Buffalo Rock, a spicy ginger ale created in 1901, continues to be produced and distributed in the city today. The other drink is a purple, grape-flavored concoction that many people consider to be the perfect complement to a loaded Birmingham hot dog: Grapico.

Grapico actually was invented in New Orleans in 1914 by the firm of J. Grossman's Sons. To promote its new drink, the company commissioned Ivan Reid and Peter de Rose, a future member of the Songwriters Hall of Fame and a hitmaker of the 1930s and 1940s, to pen a Tin Pan Alley–style song titled "Meet Me in the Land of Grapico." The tune croons about a place with grape arbor vines and air filled with sweet perfume, where love lives forever (and, presumably, where everyone drinks Grapico). The sheet music was sent free to anyone who requested it.

It took R.R. Rochell, a former grocer, to bring Grapico to Birmingham. He had been bottling the soda in the city since 1917, but he became the South's sole supplier of the drink in 1928 after Grapico's second owner, Pan American Manufacturing of New Orleans, got into legal trouble with the Federal Trade Commission. The government ruled that Pan American was guilty of deceptive advertising, implying that Grapico was made with real grapes, and barred the company from using the trademark. Rochell, however, was free to continue selling the drink and using the name. In 1940, he won federal approval for the Grapico trademark, giving him all rights to the soft drink. Buffalo Rock acquired Grapico in 1981 and has been bottling it ever since, bringing the soda into new southern markets and even introducing a diet version.

Painted wall ads for Grapico are rare, but the purple drink was enough of a draw for the owners of a restaurant at 1308 First Avenue North to promote it alongside pit barbecue, fresh-ground burgers, breakfast and, of course, hot dogs. A series of food stands served hungry diners at this location from the 1970s until 2001, but the style of the soda's logo hints that the ad appeared before 1988, the year that Buffalo Rock updated the emblem used since the drink's arrival from the "Land of Grapico."

Grapico has been bottled in Birmingham since 1917 and is considered a hometown original, even though it was developed in New Orleans. This ad for the purple drink also promotes a restaurant at 1308 First Avenue North, and it was painted between the 1970s and 1988, before the adjacent utility substation was built. *Jonathan Purvis.*

COCA-COLA

James Couden could see a lot of possibilities in a blank wall. He was a traveling Coca-Cola syrup salesman, and on a stop in Cartersville, Georgia, in 1894, he hit on a novel strategy to move more product: a free paint job for any shop that agreed to sell Coca-Cola. Of course, the newly painted wall would be a giant ad for the soft drink, but the store's name would be included as well.

This early example of the privilege system proved to be popular among retailers, who benefited from the free advertising. Couden painted the first sign himself on the side of a Cartersville pharmacy, but Coca-Cola soon hired teams of sign painters to put its logo throughout towns of every size across the country. By 1910, a quarter of the company's advertising budget was dedicated to wall signs; three years later, the figure had jumped to $259,499—far more than the allocation for any other form of advertising.

According to Mark Pendergrast, author of *For God, Country and Coca-Cola: The Unauthorized Biography of the Great American Soft Drink and the Company That Makes It*, the company had painted more than sixteen thousand wall ads by 1922. For some consumers, all of that red paint might have been just a little too much. Pendergrast recounted a Coca-Cola salesman's story from 1906 that describes a poor man "hounded almost to a state of imbecility with Coca-Cola signs." Apparently he would "wake up at night with big white devils with a red mantel chasing after him screeching, 'Coca-Cola! Coca-Cola!' until he made up his mind that he

would have to go in somewhere and get a glass of Coca-Cola or part with his reason."

The spread of the signs paralleled Coca-Cola's expansion into bottling. The first bottled Cokes appeared in 1894, the same year that the Cartersville sign was painted, but bottling didn't really take off in earnest until 1899, when Benjamin Thomas and Joseph Whitehead of Chattanooga, Tennessee, convinced Coca-Cola president Asa Candler to sell them bottling rights for one dollar. Coke bottling plants soon popped up in cities across the country.

Crawford Johnson opened the Birmingham Coca-Cola Bottling Company in 1902. Here he blended syrup and sweetener from Chattanooga with carbonated water, bottled it and shipped it out by rail or horse-drawn wagon. In the beginning, Johnson had only one other employee and a mule named Bird. Together, he and the employee could produce thirty cases of soda per hour.

According to his grandson, Allen, Crawford Johnson viewed watermelon, of all things, as his chief competitor in those early days. In the hot summers, Birmingham residents apparently eschewed Coke in favor of the juicy fruit hawked on streets throughout the city, causing sales to drop.

Painted ads for Coca-Cola decorated walls across the Birmingham area. One of the oldest might be the ad on the side of the 1887 Waters Building on Twenty-second Street North. The original occupants included Koenig and Gauche, a shop selling housekeeping necessities such as "Queen's ware" (English ceramics), on the street level and a boardinghouse upstairs. In 1900, a candy manufacturer named S. George operated his business on the first floor. If he also

Coca-Cola wall ads began popping up around the country after 1894, and this one at 211 Twenty-second Street North may date from a few years after that. The faint words around the ad are early Coca-Cola slogans; these recently disappeared under a fresh coat of paint. *Jonathan Purvis.*

sold sodas, then it's possible that the Coca-Cola ad was painted then.

The ad offers a few clues to its age. The Coca-Cola logo looks a little plump—probably the result of a sign painter interpreting the famous script. An article written by Randy Schaeffer and William Bateman in *The Coca-Cola Collectors News* notes that early painted ads differed so widely in style, color, composition and even spelling that the company began producing manuals for painters with detailed instructions on sign placement, paint colors, layout and, in particular, the depiction of the Coca-Cola name, down to the slant of the letters.

The Twenty-second Street ad also contains two of Coca-Cola's earliest slogans. "Drink Coca-Cola" appears on the first Coke wall ad in Cartersville. Another line, "Relieves Fatigue"— covered by a new coat of paint during the Waters Building's 2010–11 renovation—was used in the early years of the twentieth century and ties in with the soft drink's origin as a tonic for headaches and exhaustion. Other parts of the ad—also beneath the fresh paint—say "Sold Everywhere" and "5¢."

Birmingham and its suburbs are home to several other fading Coca-Cola ads painted over the decades. Within sight of the sign on the Waters Building is a Coke ad of a more recent vintage, painted in about 1977. Another sign, located on the back of a supermarket in Ensley, advertises Coca-Cola Classic, which debuted in the summer of 1985 after the disastrous introduction of New Coke earlier that year. A few other Coke ads remain as well, though their ages can be difficult to pinpoint because the company was diligent about keeping its walls looking fresh. Many ads were repainted annually, and some in smoky, dirty urban areas were touched up twice a year.

As for the war on watermelon, the Birmingham Coca-Cola Bottling Company finally prevailed. The business, now called Coca-Cola Bottling United, has grown into North America's third-largest bottler of Coke products. In 2011, it produced 230 million gallons for distribution in six southern states.

A whisper of an ad for Pepsi-Cola hangs on the alley wall at 109 Richard Arrington Jr. Boulevard South. Painted as early as 1907, the sign features the words "Delicious—Healthful" and "5¢" in and around the ribbon beneath the brand name. "At Founts" and "Also in Bottles" sit above the logo, out of the range of this photo. *Jonathan Purvis.*

PEPSI-COLA

Pepsi-Cola was just one of many syrup mixtures created by pharmacist Caleb Bradham in his shop in New Bern, North Carolina. In fact, it was known simply as "Brad's Drink" when it was introduced in the 1890s. The ingredient that set it apart was pepsin—at the time, a popular additive to aid digestion—which inspired the change to a catchier name.

In 1902, Bradham began selling his syrup to other soda fountains, and the drink's popularity soon attracted the attention of bottlers. By 1907, there were 40 Pepsi bottlers, including the Birmingham Pepsi-Cola Bottling Company, founded by nine North Carolinians that year. Three years later, the number of plants had jumped to 280 in twenty-four states. The soda's success also inspired copycats, including Birmingham's own Pepsin-Ola.

Two fading ads for Pepsi date from the Birmingham bottling company's early days. One sign, on the side of the old George F. Wheelock building, just two blocks from the bottler's First Avenue South location, retains just the swirling outlines of the Pepsi trademark and the faint words "At Founts—Also in Bottles." The other ad, however, has been carefully restored to look as fresh as the day it was painted on Second Avenue North.

This sign once adorned the exterior of Barber's Drug and Seed Store, which opened in 1908 in a brand-new building at the corner of Second Avenue and Twenty-fourth Street. In fact, a rough-looking faded sign for Barber's sits below the restored ad, indicating that the Pepsi sign might be an early example of a privilege. The soft drink company—or its local bottling representative—would have promoted Barber's in exchange for securing advertising space on its wall, especially if Barber's had a soda fountain like other drugstores of the era. About three years after they were painted, the Pepsi and Barber's signs vanished behind the bricks of a two-story building constructed next door for Blackwood, Bentley and Company, a seller of general merchandise, wagons, buggies, feeds and agricultural supplies.

The original Birmingham Pepsi-Cola Bottling Company also disappeared in 1911 after four years in business—just before the Pepsi-Cola Company itself faced financial difficulties and bankruptcy. The soft drink made a comeback in the 1930s, eventually paving the way for the rise of PepsiCo as an international beverage and snack food giant. A new bottler opened in Birmingham in 1938, and today the Buffalo

Another Pepsi ad at the corner of Second Avenue North and Twenty-fourth Street offers a clearer view of the soft drink's earliest local campaign. This sign appeared in about 1907, and below it, traces of an ad for the building's tenant at the time—Barber's Drug and Seed Store—remain visible. The walls of another building hid both ads for seventy years. *Jonathan Purvis.*

Rock Company oversees production and distribution of Pepsi in the region.

The Pepsi sign on Second Avenue was uncovered in the 1980s, after the former Blackwood building was replaced by a parking lot. The sign supposedly was restored at that time along with the Jack Daniel's sign on the Twenty-fourth Street façade, though the juxtaposition of bricks and paint at the top of the ad hints that much of the ad might be original. Shielded from the sun by a tree and surrounding buildings, the century-old Pepsi ad continues to look new.

ROYAL CROWN COLA

Though it has never held the market share of Coca-Cola or Pepsi, Royal Crown Cola is so familiar that it is known by its initials: RC.

Claud Hatcher, a pharmacist in Columbus, Georgia, came up with the Royal Crown name—for a ginger ale—after entering the soft drink business in 1905. The company's other products, including the cherry-flavored Chero Cola and the Nehi line of fruit-flavored drinks, became the bigger hits, however. Birmingham had bottling plants for Chero Cola/Nehi, with branches in Ensley and Bessemer, from 1913 to 1929 and Nehi alone from 1929 to 1959.

After Hatcher's death in 1933, his successors developed a new cola and named it for Hatcher's original ginger ale. Royal Crown became the company's third major soft drink success, and by 1940, it was available in forty-seven states. Today, RC Cola is available in more than forty-five countries.

In 1941, Royal Crown introduced the industry's first blind taste tests, launching the "Best by Taste Test" campaign that appeared in newspapers, in magazines and on wall ads, including this one on Gary Avenue in

the suburb of Fairfield. Celebrities including Bob Hope, Shirley Temple, Lucille Ball and Ronald Reagan endorsed the cola, which later became the first soft drink to be distributed nationally in aluminum cans. RC Cola also has long been associated with Moon Pies, another favorite southern treat, because decades ago, the combination made an affordable yet substantial snack. The duo has since been immortalized in two country songs.

During the civil rights movement, the president of Royal Crown's board of directors, a Birmingham businessman named Edward Norton, played a role in ending segregation in downtown stores. Following violent demonstrations in 1963 that saw police turn fire hoses and dogs on African American protesters, Norton and a select group of other white businessmen negotiated with protest leaders, reaching an agreement to remove racial restrictions in the stores and to hire African Americans as employees.

Birmingham had an RC bottling plant from 1934 to 1980, along with several painted ads promoting the soft drink. The Fairfield ad seems to be the only one that has survived. It sits near the edge of the business district along the town's main street, on a building that has housed a succession of restaurants, from the Roxy Sandwich Shop to Two M's (Mine & Mama's), since 1949. Layers of later ads below the RC sign highlight small local businesses specializing in color TVs and burglar bars.

Royal Crown Cola first appeared in the 1930s, but this sign at 5002 Gary Avenue in Fairfield came along after 1941, when the soft drink introduced taste tests. "Best by Taste Test" is barely visible in the yellow banner beneath the cola's name. More recent ads at the bottom of the wall promote a variety of local businesses. Jonathan Purvis.

DOUBLE COLA

When this well-preserved ad was uncovered behind a drab pile of concrete blocks, it was the visual equivalent of someone opening a shaken bottle of soda. Its vivid colors and striking design demand attention today much as they did decades ago, when Double Cola was a key competitor to Coca-Cola and Pepsi.

The Good Grape Company of Chattanooga, Tennessee, introduced Double Cola in 1920, except then it was called Marvel Cola and later, after a reformulation, Jumbo Cola. But the third time was the charm. In 1924, further tinkering with the recipe led to the debut of Double Cola. The name referred to the size of the soda's bottle and its price: Double Cola served up twelve ounces for a nickel while Coca-Cola offered six and a half ounces for the same cost. The value strategy became successful as America entered the Great Depression, and sales grew rapidly. In fact, the Double Cola Company, which followed up its successful soda with Double-Orange, Double-Lemon, Double-Grape, and Double-Dry Ginger Ale, rivaled Pepsi in size before World War II.

A Double Cola bottling plant opened in Birmingham in 1939, and the ad near the corner of Second Avenue South and Twenty-second Street might have been painted soon afterward as part of a campaign to promote the drink. At the time, the ad's wall belonged to a dry goods store run by the Tebshrany family, who had operated a market on the site since 1915. The sign enjoyed its place in the sun for only a few years, though. By 1949, it had been sealed behind concrete blocks that formed the wall of a used car lot office.

Double Cola's vibrant ad sprang back to life when a wall came down during the 2008 redevelopment of the corner at Second Avenue South and Twenty-second Street South. The sign was created after 1939, but an adjoining structure had hid it from view by the end of the 1940s. *Jonathan Purvis.*

Meanwhile, sugar shortages during World War II and a reluctance to put the cola in soda vending machines (following a failed attempt to invent the first one) reduced the Double Cola Company's ability to compete with other soft drink makers. Today, Double Cola controls less than 1 percent of an American market dominated by Coca-Cola and Pepsi. However, it has found some success in rural areas and overseas, particularly in Latin America, south Asia and the Middle East.

Back on Second Avenue South, the concrete-block wall stood until a redevelopment of the entire corner in 2008. Two nearby buildings were renovated for new tenants, and a parking lot took the place of the old used car lot, allowing the Double Cola ad to dazzle once again.

ORANGE CRUSH

On Friday, March 2, 1923, Birmingham ordered plans for a new civic auditorium, a mining company struck a deal with the state to use convicts as labor and "warfare" broke out among drivers of jitneys (privately operated passenger cars or buses) over rate reductions and increased competition. And over on Twenty-first Street South, a sign painter with the initials W.L.M. finished this ad for Orange Crush.

It's the only fading ad in town—the only one in this book, at least—with a visible artist signature and date. But it was not the only brightly colored ad for Orange Crush in the city. The beverage company was a prolific advertiser in Birmingham, according to old photographs, promoting Orange Crush as well as Lemon Crush and Lime Crush. The campaign may have begun in 1922, when an Orange Crush bottling plant opened in the city.

The Orange Crush Company, like other soft drink makers, was trying to make a big splash with the public. During the soft drink boom of the early twentieth century—and particularly during the days of prohibition—competition for the limited slots at soda fountains was fierce. An unusual flavor or ingredient could help a soda stand out and build demand, encouraging fountains to serve the drink. (One example was Birmingham's own Celery-Cola. While it might not tempt many tongues today, Celery-Cola was sold from California to Cuba in the early 1900s.)

The Orange Crush Company of Los Angeles got the bright idea to add orange

An Orange Crush ad inside a building at 105 Richard Arrington Jr. Boulevard South is unusual for two reasons: it's signed by its painter, and it looks sharp because it was exposed to the elements for only one year. The signs for the soda and Crandall Packing Company appeared in 1923; they overlap an earlier Crandall ad painted after 1917 by the Southern Ad Company. *Jonathan Purvis.*

pulp to its signature drink, encouraging consumers to equate the soda with a fresh-squeezed glass of fruit juice. The gimmick paid off because the drink has been popular ever since its introduction as "Ward's Orange Crush." It was named for Neil C. Ward, a chemist specializing in beverages who refined a formula originally invented in Chicago in 1906. Ten years later, Ward cofounded the Orange Crush Company.

W.L.M.'s ad has changed little since the day he painted it. About a year after the sign was finished, it was enclosed inside a building, preserving its color and detail. Two other ads also received protection from the elements. They mark the Birmingham location of the Crandall Packing Company, which was based in Palmyra, New York, and made sealing products, such as rubber gaskets, for engines and pumps. The earlier of the two Crandall signs, painted in blue, likely appeared soon after its building was constructed in about 1917. A credit on the wall attributes the sign to Southern Ad Company of Birmingham.

Pedestrians and motorists would not have been able to miss the Crandall sign as they crossed the long Twenty-first Street viaduct over the railroad tracks. That high visibility may have prompted Orange Crush—or its outdoor advertising representative in Birmingham—to approach Crandall about placing an ad on the wall. It's even possible that Orange Crush gave Crandall a privilege, normally a tactic used with shops and cafés that sold the soft drink. In any case, the Orange Crush ad and the second Crandall sign were painted at the same time. Evidence for this is in the design of the signs—the colors and painted frames for both complement one another.

Today, the former Crandall building, on the renamed Richard Arrington Jr. Boulevard, houses the Birmingham branch of the American Institute of Architects. The space containing the Orange Crush ad, originally built for the Foster-Alexander Corporation, a seller of mill supplies and power equipment, has been renovated and awaits a new tenant. As for W.L.M., it's impossible to say who he was or what happened to him after that March day in 1923.

CANADA DRY GINGER ALE

How did an ad for Canada Dry end up in downtown Birmingham, the hometown of the bolder, spicier Buffalo Rock ginger ale? Chalk it up to the Prohibition era, when the nation rediscovered ginger ales—and made them popular because they could be used as a mixer to hide the strong taste of bootlegged alcohol.

Canada Dry originated in Toronto, where pharmacist and chemist John McLaughlin invented it in 1904. A Birmingham bottling plant opened in 1937, but it took a little longer for the Canada Dry ad to be painted on the corner of Third Avenue North and Eighteenth Street.

This corner was a coveted location. The Publix Theatres Corporation of New York had originally planned to build the lavish Alabama Theatre there, but the owners of the small building on the spot, which housed the Goldstein Fur Company and other retailers, wouldn't sell, forcing Publix to shrink the size of the theater's lobby and reduce the number of seats from 3,500 to 2,200. By the time the movie palace opened a few doors down Third Avenue in 1927, Dewberry Drugs occupied the corner space.

Like most drugstores at the time, Dewberry had a soda fountain that catered to the crowds flocking to the Alabama to see the latest films (accompanied by the "Mighty Wurlitzer" pipe organ), as well as Broadway shows with orchestras or bands. Dewberry, a local chain founded around the turn of the twentieth century, also sold lunches, cigars and candy along with "cut-rate" drugs.

Alabama Cigar and Soda Company replaced Dewberry on the corner in the 1940s. A photograph from 1959 shows the store behind a line of people waiting to see an Audrey Hepburn movie at the Alabama, and at that time, the Canada Dry panels are blank, though adjacent ones carry ads for Hav-A-Tampa and Tampa Nugget cigars. The ads for "the Champagne of Ginger Ales" appeared between then and 1963, the soda fountain's last year of operation.

Unlike the other ads featured in this book, the Canada Dry signs are painted on glass rather than brick or metal. Bessemer sign painter Doug Watts said that glass is one of the hardest surfaces to work on because it has to be very clean and because everything must be painted on the inside of the window, in reverse.

Painted on glass, the Canada Dry ad at the corner of Third Avenue North and Eighteenth Street promotes "new low prices" on fountain drinks at Alabama Cigar and Soda Company. The sign comes from the early 1960s, when the shop was a familiar stop for patrons of the adjacent Alabama Theatre. *Jonathan Purvis.*

The Alabama Theatre and the surrounding businesses that depended on it faced many dark days as suburban movie theaters kept patrons away from downtown. In the 1980s, the Alabama chapter of the American Theater Organ Society, which had been looking after the Alabama's Wurlitzer, raised funds to buy the theater, which was under threat of being demolished and replaced with a parking lot. The group succeeded, and in 1987, the nonprofit Birmingham Landmarks took ownership. Under the direction of Cecil Whitmire, the theater underwent a full restoration and now plays host to concerts, ballet, theatrical productions and an independent film festival, as well as classic movies. In 1991, Birmingham Landmarks added the corner building to its holdings, stripping away part of the façade to reveal the Canada Dry ads.

By now you might be wondering about—or craving—the "rickey" painted on the ad. The rickey originated as an alcoholic drink, a combination of bourbon (later replaced with gin), lime and soda water. The story goes that it was concocted in Washington, D.C., in the 1880s and named for a Democratic lobbyist named Colonel Joseph Kyle Rickey. In the twentieth century, nonalcoholic versions, using sugar or syrup instead of gin and substituting other flavors for the lime, became staples of soda fountains across the country.

clear spring waters as a key ingredient. So why does a fading ad on Second Avenue North claim Birmingham as the headquarters of the legendary whiskey maker? And why is Jack's name misspelled?

The story begins not with Jack himself, but with the Motlow brothers—Lemuel ("Lem"), John Franklin ("Spoons"), Jesse Butler and Thomas—all nephews of the legendary distiller. In 1903, the Motlows announced the construction of a one-hundred-bushel whiskey distillery in Alabama that would be one of the largest and most modern in the country. The next year, the Motlow Distilling Company opened at 1215 Avenue B (now Second Avenue South) in Birmingham, with Spoons as president and Jesse as vice-president, secretary and master distiller.

The company letterhead promotes East Lake corn whiskey and Jefferson County rye whiskey, as well as Tennessee Lincoln County whiskey (Jack Daniel's original whiskey). The Motlows also operated a smaller distillery and saloon in Gadsden, Alabama, that specialized in Coosa River corn whiskey. The passage of county prohibition laws forced the closure of both distilleries in 1908.

JACK DANIEL'S

The Jack Daniel Distillery has made its hometown of Lynchburg, Tennessee, an integral part of its brand image, extolling the area's

This misspelled ad highlights the wanderings of the famous Jack Daniel's distillery after Tennessee voted to ban alcohol production in 1911. The company was actually headquartered in Birmingham for the next four years, though the building with the sign at 2331 Second Avenue North did not house the main office. *Jonathan Purvis.*

The situation shifted over the next few years, however. By 1911, Jefferson County had changed its mind and voted to allow alcohol sales. Tennessee, on the other hand, had passed a statewide prohibition law. Jack Daniel also died in October of that year, leaving his company to his nephew Lem.

The dutiful Lem reopened the Birmingham plant as the Jack Daniel Distilling Company, producing his uncle's famous "Old No. 7" whiskey, as well as his own corn whiskey. He also served as president of the Jack Daniel Distributing Company, located at 2431 Second Avenue North.

Around the same time, Lem opened a distillery in St. Louis, which proved to be a prescient move. In 1915, when Alabama followed Tennessee's lead and went dry statewide, Lem shut down the Birmingham distillery and relocated all operations to the Missouri plant. That distillery closed down just ahead of national prohibition a few years later. Jack Daniel's whiskey wouldn't be produced again until 1937, when the repeal of federal and state laws allowed the company to resume distilling in Lynchburg.

Artifacts from Jack Daniel's stay in Birmingham are rare. While glass whiskey bottles embossed with the city's name are highly prized among collectors, the fading ad on the corner of Second Avenue North and Twenty-fourth Street is the most visible reminder. It originally was painted between 1911 and 1915, when the Jack Daniel Distributing Company was located one block down the street. The ad decorated the façade of Barber's Department Store, which had begun as a drugstore and also sold seed and hardware.

The Jack Daniel's ad, along with the early Pepsi-Cola sign on the opposite façade of the building, was probably restored in the late 1980s, when the structure's exterior was repaired and painted. Today, the corner building houses a jewelry store and screenprinting shop.

As for the odd misspelling of Jack's name, no one really knows why it's wrong. Perhaps the sign painter got a little too close to the advertised product one day.

CREAM OF KENTUCKY

Whenever a brick building went up on a street corner in Birmingham's first few decades, it most likely housed a saloon or a grocery store—or a combination of both. In fact, a saloon occupied one of the first four buildings to appear after the city's founding, according to the Hawkins letter mentioned in the Services chapter. It's easy to see why these watering holes were so popular; in a city full of young, often rural and poorly paid laborers who spent long hours working tough jobs, the saloons offered brief escapes. In 1900, according to a book produced by the Birmingham-Jefferson Historical Society, the city had ninety-eight saloons (and only forty churches).

The sign painters for Cream of Kentucky bourbon likely didn't know that the three-story building at the corner of Second Avenue South and Twenty-second Street had once been a saloon. It probably was chosen for its high visibility instead. But the structure's history makes its façade a fitting place to sell liquor.

Along with the words "Cream of Kentucky," this ad once featured the illustration of a bourbon bottle, now barely visible just below the letter "C." The sign, which might have been painted as early as the 1930s, blends with other ads for Bull Durham smoking tobacco and Uneeda Biscuit on the back of the building at 200 Twenty-second Street South. *Jonathan Purvis.*

Though the building might have been constructed as early as 1888, Daniel Eyer Jr. opened a saloon and grocery store at the corner in about 1895, using the rooms above as his residence. (The upper floors also served as a boardinghouse.) The space remained a saloon until 1910, selling soft drinks for the last two years while Jefferson County's prohibition laws were in effect.

While we don't know what Eyer's saloon looked like inside, Birmingham saloons ran the gamut from dive bars to elegant establishments for gentlemen. One in downtown Birmingham even featured marble floors, a copper chandelier and a mirror thirty-two feet long. Many saloons served meals along with drinks and sold Louisiana lottery tickets.

County, state and national prohibition laws ended the reign of saloons in Birmingham, forcing many to sell soft drinks or ice cream or close altogether. The anti-alcohol regulations didn't kill a certain distillery in Franklin County, Kentucky, however. Its savvy leader, a man appropriately named Colonel Albert Bacon Blanton, had joined the distillery in 1897 as a sixteen-year-old office boy. Five years later, he was running the entire plant, and when national prohibition rolled around in 1920, the whiskey wunderkind convinced the federal government to allow the distillery to continue production. (Only four in the country won the right to remain open and produce whiskey for medicinal purposes.) After the repeal of prohibition in 1933, Blanton's distillery, then owned by Schenley Distillers Corporation of New York, began producing Cream of Kentucky bourbon.

Schenley's promotional campaign for the "double rich" bourbon featured print ads illustrated by Norman Rockwell along with painted walls. Two ads went up on the building at Second Avenue South and Twenty-second Street. One, with the words "Cream of Kentucky," faces south; today, most motorists on the street don't see it because traffic flows in one direction past it. The other, more obvious ad appears on the western façade. There, the brand name once shared the wall with a tall illustration of the bourbon bottle, which is barely visible today.

The building's prominent location meant that several advertisers painted its walls over the years. In fact, the Cream of Kentucky signs probably are the most recent additions. A large ad for Nabisco fronts the Second Avenue side, while the back shows evidence of a Uneeda Biscuit sign where the bourbon ad sits today. Traces of a Bull Durham ad are there as well.

Since its heyday as a saloon, the corner building has housed paint and sheet metal shops, a bakery and café and, finally, a series of car-related businesses as Birmingham's Automotive District developed around it. Cream of Kentucky has disappeared, however, ceasing production in 1982, but Blanton's distillery survives under a different name and continues to produce a variety of bourbons.

National Brands

By the turn of the twentieth century, improvements in transportation and manufacturing had expanded the scale of production and the range of destinations where many consumer goods could be shipped, enabling the development of nationally known and nationally sold products. In Birmingham, the railroads that had laid the foundation for the city's rise as an industrial center also made it a key distribution point for consumer goods. Many major companies—from meat processors to elevator manufacturers—established regional offices here to connect with wholesalers, retailers and the public.

At the same time, the evolution of advertising agencies laid the groundwork for massive national promotional campaigns that put the same message in newspapers, magazines, streetcar ads, walls and more—anywhere the consumer was likely to look. Catchy slogans and memorable images encouraged the public to associate products with positive attributes and feelings, giving rise to the concept of the brand.

Outdoor advertising played a particularly important role in helping to herald the advance of the new offerings throughout the country. With their visibility, painted walls helped many brands to become familiar household names. Today, it's rare to find an American town—even in the most rural areas—that doesn't have a barn or brick wall with traces of an ad for tobacco, flour, snacks, shortening, medicine or another necessity from the era.

BULL DURHAM SMOKING TOBACCO

When it came to advertising, Bull Durham smoking tobacco was like, well, a bull in a china shop. Developed in Durham, North Carolina, in the wake of the Civil War, the Bull Durham brand had a national campaign underway by 1877. And these were not subtle ads. A bull, often depicted in full color and in all of his well-endowed glory, appeared in gigantic form on walls across the country, accompanied by letters several feet high spelling out the brand name. According to legend, the bull was even painted on an Egyptian pyramid.

W.T. Blackwell and Company, which owned Bull Durham, was a branding pioneer, using the bull in different forms of advertising, as well

Birmingham's largest fading ad belongs to Bull Durham smoking tobacco. It was part of a massive advertising campaign that blanketed the country with ads for "the Old Reliable," and it showed up on the wall at 1711 First Avenue North after 1911. Later ads for Sloan's Liniment, Uneeda Biscuit, Dixie Cycle & Toy Company and Cook Credit Furniture overlap the block-wide tobacco ad. *Jonathan Purvis.*

as on the tobacco packaging itself, creating an instant connection in the minds of consumers. But why a bull? When J.R. Green, the creator of the tobacco blend, was searching for a name and trademark, a friend pointed him to the bull on a jar of Colman's mustard, which he thought came from Durham, England, and an icon was born.

Bull Durham grew into one of the world's most famous trademarks and a leader in tobacco sales. Meanwhile, competitor James B. Duke was busy dominating the cigarette market and managing the rise of the American Tobacco Company, which monopolized the industry. In 1898, Duke brought the W.T. Blackwell Company and Bull Durham into his fold.

In a 1911 antitrust ruling, the United States Supreme Court broke up Duke's monopoly into three companies. The now smaller American Tobacco Company retained Bull Durham and continued blanketing the country with its giant painted ads, promoting the tobacco as an option for smokers who wanted to roll their own cigarettes. On First

Avenue North in Birmingham, the company painted a sign spanning an entire city block on the side of a new building, then home to the William Wise wholesale liquor firm. The massive letters, painted in yellow and white on a dark background, proclaim Bull Durham to be "the Standard of the World," "the Old Reliable" and "the Best for Three Generations." An image of the product itself, shown wrapped in cloth with its label and seals, remains on the wall. No evidence proves that the famous bull was part of this ad, but it may lie under the painted signs added to the wall in later decades.

Other Bull Durham ads loomed over Birmingham's streets. A portion of one remains inside a residential loft farther down First Avenue North, decorating a wall once visible from the street, but most have faded out of sight. American Tobacco Company also placed Bull Durham ads in baseball parks around the country, leading some people to believe that the brand inspired the name of the "bullpen," the warm-up area for relief pitchers.

As ready-made cigarettes rose in popularity, Bull Durham was eclipsed by other American Tobacco brands such as Lucky Strike. Production of the legendary tobacco moved out of North Carolina in 1957.

The giant Birmingham ad had an even shorter lifespan. Sign painters covered it with at least two ads for Sloan's Liniment and another for Uneeda Biscuit. For several decades after 1937, a one-story auto garage next door obscured the lower halves of all the signs on the wall. The Bull Durham ad reemerged as the newer ads faded, and today it overlooks a parking lot, offering a panoramic view of the city's largest ghost sign.

TUXEDO TOBACCO

Tobacco companies, along with patent medicine makers, were among the most prolific of the early national advertisers. Painted ads appeared on brick walls in the cities and on the sides and roofs of barns in rural areas—even on rocks in the wilderness. In addition to Bull Durham, major tobacco advertisers included Star Tobacco ("a Thought in Every Chew"), Mail Pouch, Owl Cigars and Tuxedo Tobacco.

While Birmingham once had ads for most of these companies, a sign for Tuxedo survives inside the Wooster Lofts. It was painted between 1910, when the wall was built as the exterior of a neighboring warehouse, and 1923, when the loft building was constructed as the Wood-Fruitticher grocery warehouse. Today, "Tuxedo" is visible in one of the lofts, while "Tobacco" appears a floor below—in the same unit that includes half of the Gold Dust Twins. (We'll meet them later in this chapter.)

The R.A. Patterson Tobacco Company of Richmond, Virginia, produced Tuxedo Tobacco, a blend that Patterson, a physician, had developed in the years after the Civil War. A newspaper ad from 1913 claims that the good doctor "put his scientific mind to work on the problem" after friends swore off pipe smoking due to sensitive mouths and throats. The resulting Tuxedo blend removed "all the bite and sting" and became popular—even winning the endorsement of athletes. In the same ad, American sportsmen fresh from the 1912 Stockholm Olympics declared Tuxedo Tobacco to be enjoyable and beneficial. Shotputter "Pat" McDonald said that it made him feel stronger, and marathon runner

Two floors of a residential building at 2321 First Avenue North split Birmingham's only remaining Tuxedo Tobacco ad. ("Tuxedo" is in the unit above the one pictured here.) It appeared between 1910 and 1923, but an ad for Gold Dust Washing Powder clips off the "O" at the end, indicating that the Tuxedo sign already had outlived its usefulness. *Jonathan Purvis.*

Gaston Strobino added that Tuxedo "never hurts my mind." Other ads, including painted ones, promoted Tuxedo as "the pipe smoke for gentlemen" and declared, "We made it best. Its friends made it famous."

The R.A. Patterson Tobacco Company became part of Duke's American Tobacco Company trust soon after the turn of the twentieth century. While Tuxedo eventually faded in popularity, another former Patterson brand—a cigarette called Lucky Strike—became a hit.

UNEEDA BISCUIT/NATIONAL BISCUIT COMPANY

In the nineteenth century, snacking on crackers was akin to a game of chance. If you were lucky, you got fresh, crisp, tasty morsels, but if the baking gods did not smile on you, a bag of stale, broken, soggy and even smelly crackers might be your fate.

It all depended on the cracker barrel. Back then, crackers were sold straight from the barrels and boxes they arrived in, which usually were placed on the floors of dusty, dirty general stores and markets. When a customer wanted crackers, shopkeepers would scoop the snacks into a bag and sell them by volume. Naturally, the crackers near the top of the barrel were the freshest and best. Those toward the bottom were more questionable—and likely already nibbled on by mice and insects. To make matters worse, the cracker barrels were used multiple times. Empty ones went back to bakeries, which refilled them and returned them to stores.

The National Biscuit Company ended that unsanitary era in 1899 with Uneeda Biscuit, a soda cracker enveloped in waxed paper inside a cardboard carton. This "In-er-seal" packaging sparked a revolution in the food industry, changing the way foods were produced, distributed and sold, as well as helping to pave the way for the modern supermarket.

Henry McKinney of N. W. Ayer and Son, the company's advertising agency, came up with the product's punny name. Rejecting suggestions that included Pherenice, Trim, Dandelo, Fireside and Bisco, McKinney wrote that the name had to be "simple, plain, and novel." Once they had selected Uneeda, company president Adolphus Green chose "Biscuit" over "Cracker" because, as a British term, it represented a higher-quality product far removed from the soggy mess at the bottom of cracker barrels.

Uneeda launched an ambitious branding campaign—perhaps the largest the country had seen and one of the first to promote an entirely new product. Teaser ads asking, "Do you know Uneeda Biscuit?" covered the country, from newspapers, magazines, posters, banners, theater programs and window displays to streetcars, billboards and painted walls. The witty campaign had the desired impact. Suddenly, the public demanded Uneeda Biscuit.

Later ads featured a five-year-old boy dressed in a classic fisherman's coat and hat, carrying a box of Uneeda Biscuits, which gave the product an indelible trademark and reminded customers of the "In-er-seal" packaging. The cracker's cartons proclaimed that Uneeda could be "Served with every meal; take a box with you on your travels; splendid for sandwiches; perfect for picnics; unequalled for general use; do not contain sugar. This is a perfect food for everybody, and the price places them within the reach of all."

In 1900, a year after its introduction, Uneeda sales exceeded 10 million a month. The product had become a fixture of everyday life, so much so that a writer for the journal *Printers' Ink* called Uneeda an "agent of Americanization" for new immigrants. Naturally, the cracker spawned a host of competing snacks with names such as Uwanta, Ulika and Iwanta—all attempting to cash in on Uneeda's popularity. (Uneeda's competitors also painted walls, and a partial ad for Takhoma Biscuit survives in Bessemer.)

The success of Uneeda enabled the National Biscuit Company to live up to its name, giving its member bakeries a common product and a national brand. The company, eventually known as Nabisco, was born in an age of consolidation and monopolization in nearly every industry, from oil, steel and tobacco down to the manufacture of radiators and matches. Toward the end of the 1880s, large bakeries in cities across the country began merging as a strategy to improve efficiency, upgrade technology, expand distribution and share costs. In 1898,

Uneeda Biscuit peeks out from behind later signs on the First Avenue North wall that also hosts the giant Bull Durham ad. The promotion for "the Perfect Soda Cracker" was painted between 1911 and 1918, when the National Biscuit Company's "In-er-seal" logo changed. *Jonathan Purvis.*

following a "biscuit war" that presaged the Coke-Pepsi battles of the 1980s, three of the nation's largest baking companies and a group of smaller bakeries combined to form Nabisco. The *New York Times* reported that the deal brought "all the biscuit and cracker companies between Salt Lake City on the west; Portland,

Maine, on the east; and St. Louis and New Orleans in the south" under one management. At its founding, Nabisco had 114 plants and the capacity to produce 360 million pounds of crackers per year.

Dozens other Nabisco brands followed in Uneeda's wake, from Fig Newtons and Animal Crackers to Premium Saltines, Lorna Doone cookies, Oyster Crackers and Mallomars. Vanilla Wafers appeared in 1901 (along with lemon, orange, chocolate and mint versions), and Oreo came along in 1912. All were sold in the In-er-seal packaging.

Remnants of Uneeda and Nabisco ads linger on walls throughout the country. The most prominent one in Birmingham is part of a series of signs on the eastern façade of 1711 First

The Uneeda Biscuit ad at the intersection of Second Avenue South and Twenty-second Street may have been a ghost sign as early as the 1930s. A photograph from that time shows that the bottom of the sign is cut off, much like it is today, concealing the National Biscuit Company name. ("Uneeda Biscuit" appeared on the back of the building at one time.) The faint words on the horizontal strip of bricks below the Uneeda ad promote Ranger Motor Sales Company, located down the block in 1920. *Jonathan Purvis.*

Avenue North. It came along after the giant Bull Durham ad and probably at the same time as a neighboring Sloan's Liniment sign. The Uneeda ad likely appeared before 1918, when Nabisco's logo changed slightly from the one on the wall, and it definitely was there by 1937, when an auto garage constructed next door cut off the lower portion of the sign for a few decades. In 1985, about half of the Uneeda ad disappeared under new painted ads for Dixie Cycle and Toy Company and Cook Credit Furniture, though the older paint has begun to show through in recent years.

The text of the First Avenue Uneeda sign reads, "The Perfect Soda Cracker" and "Sold Only in Packages," and includes the five-cent price and National Biscuit Company name. The ad also features the Nabisco trademark, which company lore ascribes to founding president Green. In *Out of the Cracker Barrel: The Nabisco Story from Animal Crackers to Zuzus*, William Cahn wrote that Green discovered the mark in "an ancient volume containing medieval Italian printers' symbols. One of them was a cross with two bars and an oval, representing—so it said—the triumph of the moral and spiritual over the evil and the material," which is lot of responsibility for a box of crackers.

Across the railroad tracks, another Uneeda/Nabisco ad faces Second Avenue South on a building situated at the intersection with Twenty-second Street. The Uneeda portion once ran along the back wall but now has faded and mixed together with other ads for Cream of Kentucky bourbon and Bull Durham smoking tobacco. The rest of the Nabisco ad proclaims the company "The King of Wheat Foods" and includes the nickel

price and the company's In-er-seal trademark. Depending on how the paint has weathered over the years, the current sign could have been created *before* the version of the ad shown in a photograph of the building from the late 1930s, which carries the slogan "The National Soda Cracker."

Nabisco freshened up its walls each year. Cahn explained that on any given working day, a painting crew was at work on a Nabisco ad somewhere in the country. "The crew started out each year at Christmas, covered the entire South, and swung back like birds of passage about the first of April," he wrote. Green insisted that the names "Uneeda" and "National Biscuit Company" appear in the same font and size in every wall ad.

As Nabisco introduced new brands over the decades, Uneeda slowly faded in popularity. In 2008, Nabisco, by then a part of Kraft Foods, discontinued the venerable cracker, whose cartons still carried the image of the boy in the yellow fisherman's slicker.

SLOAN'S LINIMENT

Many a Birmingham worker turned to a bottle of Sloan's Liniment after a long day of work in the mines or mills. One of the patent medicines from the early twentieth century that actually lived up to its claims, Sloan's could soothe and warm sore or stiff muscles when applied to the skin.

The remedy initially was advertised as being "good for man or beast" because it was invented by a veterinarian as a treatment for horses. Dr. Andrew Sloan's medicine had become well

Ivy covers part of a Sloan's Liniment ad on the side of 2308 Second Avenue North during the summer months. Painted soon after the turn of the twentieth century, the ad showcased the pain reliever that was "good for man or beast." *Jonathan Purvis.*

known around his hometown of Zanesville, Ohio, in the late 1800s, but sales multiplied once people discovered that it helped their own aches and pains. In 1903, Earl Sloan, one of Andrew's sons, founded a company in Boston to manufacture and market the product nationally. He called himself "Doctor" Sloan and put his face—with a stylish bow tie and handlebar mustache—on the label of every bottle.

Patent medicine makers during that time were eager advertisers, and Sloan's was no different. The company's painted ads were huge, often spanning the side of a building. Sloan's also bought ad space in newspapers and magazines and produced collectible trade cards and promotional giveaways (including its *Cook*

Book and Advice to Housekeepers, offering hints on health, child care, etiquette and poultry raising). Sloan's promoted its liniment as a treatment for rheumatism, arthritis and lumbago, as well as strains and sprains. One newspaper ad even touted it as an antiseptic that could heal cuts and burns and "draw the poison from the sting of insects." Remarkably, Sloan's Liniment is still produced today, even though it is no longer a household name.

One place where the Sloan's name still occupies a position of prominence is this wall on Second Avenue North—for part of the year, at least. During the warmer months, ivy obscures half of the fading ad, leaving only "Liniment" visible. Below the brand name, the words "Kills Pain" are barely readable.

When this ad was painted—most likely following the national rollout of Sloan's in the early 1900s—Second Avenue had recently undergone a transformation. Substantial brick stores had replaced wooden houses and empty lots. This new part of town was racially mixed, with grocery stores, general merchandise retailers, saloons and boardinghouses for both African American and white customers. In fact, one of the first occupants of the two-story building behind the Sloan's ad was an African American woman named Eliza Johnson. In the early 1890s, she operated a restaurant and boardinghouse in the building and lived upstairs.

Through the years, the building has housed a grocery, a barber, a clothing shop, cook shops, shoemakers, a hatter and Era Dickerson's saloon, while the second floor provided space for furnished rooms and retailers. At least one tenant, Red's Cleaners and Dyers, covered the brick front of the building in painted text advertising its prices and "Suits Pressed While U Wait" in the 1930s. No traces of these signs remain.

Recently, Second Avenue has experienced another transformation, with new shops and restaurants revitalizing the formerly vacant, run-down historic buildings. This building is, once again, a saloon of sorts, promising a different kind of liquid relief than the fading ad playing peekaboo in the ivy.

GOLD DUST WASHING POWDER

The late nineteenth century was a dirty era, particularly in smoky, sooty, grimy industrial cities such as Birmingham. It's no surprise, then, that soap products were in high demand, and soap manufacturers were eager advertisers, looking for any way to make their brands memorable.

Gold Dust washing powder was an all-purpose cleaner introduced by the N.K. Fairbank Company of Chicago in the 1880s—perfect for dishes, laundry, silverware, windows, floors and woodwork, according to its print ads. But the yellow powder really set itself apart from the competition with the arrival of its two trademark characters, the Gold Dust Twins.

Today, the sight of "Goldie" and "Dustie" is quite shocking, and there's no doubt that they blatantly encapsulate dated, negative stereotypes of African Americans as children, servants and primitive people. Marilyn Kern-Foxworth, author of *Aunt Jemima, Uncle Ben, and Rastus: Blacks in Advertising, Yesterday, Today, and Tomorrow*, wrote that the condescending racial overtones accompanied the twins from their birth. "The idea came from a cartoon in the English humor magazine *Punch*, showcasing two black children

A relic of racist advertising lingers inside a loft at 2321 First Avenue North. The Gold Dust Twins were the popular mascots for Gold Dust Washing Powder for decades after their introduction in the 1880s. This mural went up between 1910 and 1923, when the current loft building hid it from public view. *Jonathan Purvis.*

The other Gold Dust Twin hovers in a stairwell of the First Avenue loft building, separated from his sibling by a wall. *Jonathan Purvis.*

characters performing the tasks ascribed to the washing powder.

The half-naked boys in skirts, along with the slogan "Let the Gold Dust Twins do your work," became American advertising icons, showing up on walls, in magazines and newspapers and on promotional items ranging from calendars and tin containers to thermometers, mirrors and even a children's coloring book. Young actors portrayed the twins at the 1904 St. Louis World's Fair, and in 1925, they had their own *Amos 'n' Andy*–style radio show, where they were voiced by white performers.

Goldie and Dustie washed dishes high above First Avenue North in Birmingham. Their ad was painted on the outer wall of the City Paper Company warehouse constructed in about 1910, overlapping another mural for Tuxedo Tobacco. Both ads disappeared from public view in about 1923, when the new Wood-Fruitticher wholesale grocery warehouse was attached to the City Paper building. Both the soap and the twins had receded from national prominence by the middle of the century.

In 1986, the Wood-Fruitticher building, by then a warehouse for Calder Furniture, became Wooster Lofts, the city's first residential loft development. The ad featuring the Gold Dust Twins remains sharp and bright, which indicates that it had not been exposed to the elements for many years before it was enclosed in the building. Unfortunately, a wall now separates the twins. Goldie and the box of washing powder, protected by sealer, are inside a private residence, while Dustie and a sink full of dishes linger in a stairwell, providing a flashback to an era that was dirty in more ways than one.

washing each other in a tub," she explained. "The caption read, 'Warranted to wash clean and not fade.'" The image of the bathing twins began appearing on the Gold Dust packages by 1887, and around the turn of the century, N.K. Fairbank hired well-known American illustrator E.W. Kemble to turn them into cartoon

ADAMS TUTTI-FRUTTI PEPSIN GUM

Thomas Adams Sr. is considered the father of modern chewing gum, but the guy who really got the gumball rolling was the Mexican general Antonio Lopez de Santa Anna—the same one who stormed the Alamo and massacred Davy Crockett and its other defenders. By 1869, Santa Anna had helped Mexico win independence from Spain, lost a war with Texas, served as Mexico's president and dictator and gone into exile. He eventually ended up in Staten Island, New York, plotting ways to raise a fortune so that he could build an army to regain power in Mexico.

Santa Anna was convinced that he could get rich by creating a rubber substitute or additive using chicle, the dried sap of the Mexican sapodilla tree. After crossing paths with Adams, a New York inventor and glass merchant, the general presented him with the challenge and some chicle he had brought from Mexico.

After a year of working with chicle, Adams's only discovery was that it could never work as a rubber replacement because it simply wasn't elastic or resilient enough. Adams was about to abandon his efforts to make chicle useful when he visited a drugstore and saw a girl buy chewing gum, at that time made from paraffin wax. The inventor knew that Mexicans chewed chicle, and he had done it himself during his experiments, so that night, he and his four sons boiled and kneaded the chicle to create chewing gum as we know it today. The first batch was branded as "Adams' New York Gum No. 1—Snapping and Stretching," and was sold in drugstores at two pieces for a penny.

The Adams gum was an instant hit and prompted the development of sweetened and flavored gums, including the fruit-based Tutti-Frutti, one of the first gums promoted in a large advertising campaign and one of the first sold in vending machines. Competitors sprang up, including Dr. Edward Beeman, a druggist in Cleveland, Ohio, who had developed a pepsin powder to remedy indigestion. He then figured out how to combine it with chicle, creating pepsin gum, which supposedly was beneficial for the chewer's health. (Robert Hendrickson, in *The Great American Chewing Gum Book*, revealed that there is little evidence that pepsin gum actually aids digestion.) Adams began adding pepsin to its gums by the 1890s, shortly before it and Beeman joined other gum makers in the American Chicle Company trust.

Adams and its competitors, particularly Wrigley, invested heavily in outdoor advertising across the country. In Birmingham, a two-story-high ad for Tutti-Frutti scored a prime spot on First Avenue North, highly visible to anyone crossing into downtown on the long viaduct over the railroad tracks from Sloss Furnaces and the eastern neighborhoods. The ad's focal point is a detailed illustration of a pack of peppermint-flavored gum, complete with Tutti-Frutti's unusual trademark, a pair of hands playing the card game euchre. The rest of the large ad spells out the Adams and Tutti-Frutti names in giant letters.

The gum ad was painted on the side of the Martin Biscuit Company bakery between 1910, when that building was constructed, and 1920, when the exterior wall became the interior of the Hinkle Brothers roofing company. Later, the space housed a cigar company, a grocery store and a dish and

The hands holding cards in this gum ad highlight the sign painter's attention to detail—especially considering that most people would not have seen the ad up close. Adams Tutti-Frutti Pepsin Gum placed its sign on the east wall of 2425 First Avenue North between 1910 and 1920. The ad now decorates the interior of the building next door. *Jonathan Purvis.*

glassware retailer. In 2012, the building's new owner began renovating the building with plans to preserve the Tutti-Frutti ad.

The Adams name continued to appear on several brands of gums until recently, when Cadbury Adams merged with Kraft Foods. While pepsin gum and Tutti-Frutti have fallen out of favor, the industry Thomas Adams created now brings in billions of dollars each year—a fortune far beyond the wildest dreams of the scheming Santa Anna.

GEORGE A. HORMEL

Birmingham and Alabama have always loved sitting down to a heaping plate of pork— preferably served as a slab of ribs bathed in barbecue sauce or as sausages accompanying a buttermilk biscuit. It was a market that spawned several homegrown pork processors, but outside companies were eager to sink their teeth into it as well.

George A. Hormel, a veteran of Chicago's meat packinghouses, founded his namesake company in Austin, Minnesota, in 1891, focusing on pork products. By the early twentieth century, Hormel had opened distribution centers in cities across the Midwest and South. The Birmingham location opened on First Avenue North in 1922, taking over a three-story warehouse formerly occupied by the Franklin, Stiles and Franklin Grocery Company. The building also had an entrance on Morris Avenue, facilitating transportation by train and truck.

It was a good time to be a pork processor. In the 1920s and 1930s, Hormel introduced canned ham, beef stew, chili and the infamous luncheon meat known as SPAM. In Birmingham, the 2300 block of First Avenue North became a mini meatpacking district, with five processing facilities, including Chicago's Armour and Company and local competitor A.C. Legg.

Hormel painted an ad on the outside wall of its building, which at that time faced an empty lot. The green text below the company name reads "Dairy Brand," the label for a line

of products that included ham, bacon, sausage and even smoked tongue and lard. The company promoted the popular brand through recipe books that offered "toothsome recipes" and "dainty ways" of serving ham.

In about 1936, Wood-Fruitticher built an annex to its grocery warehouse that concealed the Hormel ad. Just a few years later, in the early 1940s, Hormel moved out and was replaced by another meatpacking company, Star Provision

The full text of this ad reads "Geo. A. Hormel Dairy Brand," and it marks the site of the company's Birmingham distribution center, which opened at 2327 First Avenue North in 1922. Painted before 1936, the sign outlived the structure it adorned, which was demolished in the 1980s. Now it hangs on inside a loft in the neighboring building. *Jonathan Purvis.*

Company, which made sausages and products under the Delicious brand. The building later became a storage warehouse for Calder Furniture before it was torn down in 1982.

Fortunately, the exterior wall of the Hormel building had been used as the interior wall of the neighboring Wood-Fruitticher warehouse. When that space was converted into Birmingham's first residential loft development, the Hormel sign was preserved. In the meantime, Hormel itself became an international brand; today, the company sells its products in more than forty countries.

Kentucky, as well as the location of its Birmingham branch.

Founded in 1880, the company claimed to be the South's largest flour mill as well as the world's largest winter wheat mill. It distributed "Always Reliable" Obelisk Flour throughout several states, and its Egyptian-style logo, complete with camel, pyramid and Sphinx, adorned barrels, sacks and advertising from the beginning. Samuel Thruston Ballard, one of the two brothers who founded the company, had an affinity for ancient Egypt; in 1904, he purchased a 2,500-year-old mummy to display in Louisville's public library.

BALLARD & BALLARD

Egyptology meets poultry in a curious ad promoting two of the best-known products of the Ballard & Ballard Company of Louisville,

Between 1923 and the late 1930s, Ballard & Ballard Company sold its Obelisk Flour and Insurance Feeds for farm animals from this location at 2409 First Avenue South. ("Birmingham Branch" is barely visible above the Obelisk logo.) The ads reappeared in the 2000s following the demolition of a neighboring building. *Jonathan Purvis.*

Ballard also catered to farmers, creating Insurance Feeds for chickens and dairy cows. The company claimed that the mixture, which listed buttermilk as an ingredient, "insured" that the hens would be healthy and productive.

The building on First Avenue South housing Ballard's Birmingham wholesalers was constructed in 1910. The company's local offices moved here in 1923 from a downtown location, and it's likely that the painted hen—and Sphinx—came to roost on this wall soon afterward.

Ballard vacated the space in about 1937, and over the decades, it became a warehouse for mining equipment, wire rope and insulation. A glass company later used it for the fabrication and storage of windows. Next door, a building went up that obscured the ads for many years until it was torn down in about 2005. Today, the renovated Ballard branch houses both a landscape architecture firm and a private residence, and the double ad serves as a colorful landmark on the street.

As for Ballard & Ballard, it was purchased by Pillsbury in 1950, but its legacy lives on in supermarkets across America. In 1931, Ballard bought a Louisville company that was the first to develop canned, refrigerated dough. Ballard's Oven-Ready Biscuits, advertised in national women's magazines, became a hit and helped pave the way for hundreds of ready-to-bake goods, from cinnamon rolls to cookie dough, that we enjoy today.

Bibliography

Books

Atkins, Leah Rawls. *The Valley and the Hills: An Illustrated History of Birmingham and Jefferson County.* 2nd ed. Woodland Hills, CA: Windsor Publications, 1996.

Baggett, James L. *Historic Photos of Birmingham.* Nashville, TN: Turner Publishing Company, 2006.

Barnes, Michael B. "The Thomas Jefferson Hotel: An Art Historical Review." *Papers on Some Buildings of Birmingham.* Birmingham: University of Alabama at Birmingham Department of Art, 1994.

Barton, Jessica L. *Historic Photos of Birmingham in the 50s, 60s and 70s.* Nashville, TN: Turner Publishing Company, 2006.

Basten, Fred E. *Great American Billboards.* Berkeley, CA: Ten Speed Press, 2007.

Bennett, James R. *Historic Birmingham and Jefferson County: An Illustrated History.* San Antonio, TX: Historical Publishing Network, 2008.

Birmingham city directories. Various publishers, 1883–2010.

Birmingham Historical Society. *Downtown Discovery Tour.* 3rd ed. Birmingham, AL: self-published, 2001.

Birmingham's Lebanese: "The Earth Turned to Gold." Birmingham, AL: Birmingfind, 1981.

Birmingham telephone directories. Various publishers, 1925–1980.

Birmingham Year Book 1920. Birmingham, AL: Birmingham Civic Association, 1920.

Bowsher, Alice Meriwether, Philip A. Morris and Marjorie Longenecker White. *Cinderella Stories: Transformations of Historic Birmingham Buildings.* Birmingham, AL: Birmingham Historical Society, 1990.

Burkhardt, Ann McCorquodale. "Town Within a City: The Five Points South Neighborhood 1880–1930." *Journal of the Birmingham Historical Society* 7, nos. 3 and 4 (November 1982). Edited by Alice Meriwether Bowsher.

Cahn, William. *Out of the Cracker Barrel: The Nabisco Story from Animal Cracker to Zuzus.* New York: Simon and Schuster, 1969.

Cruikshank, George M. *A History of Birmingham and Its Environs: A Narrative Account of Their Historical Progress, Their People, and Their Principal Interests.* Vol. 2. New York: Lewis Publishing Company, 1920.

DuBose, John Witherspoon. *Jefferson County and Birmingham, Alabama: Historical and Biographical.* Birmingham, AL: Caldwell Printing Works, 1887.

Fede, Frank Joseph. *Italians in the Deep South: Their Impact on Birmingham and the American Heritage.* Montgomery, AL: Black Belt Press, 1994.

Fleming, David B., and Mary Allison Haynie. *Ensley and Tuxedo Junction.* Charleston, SC: Arcadia Publishing, 2011.

Garrow, David. *Bearing the Cross: Martin Luther King, Jr., and the Southern Christian Leadership Conference.* New York: HarperCollins, 2004.

Gudis, Catherine. *Buyways: Billboards, Automobiles, and the American Landscape.* New York: Routledge, 2004.

Haas, Cynthia Lea. *Ghost Signs of Arkansas.* Fayetteville: University of Arkansas Press, 1997.

Hendrickson, Robert. *The Great American Chewing Gum Book.* Radnor, PA: Chilton Book Company, 1976.

Henley, John C., Jr. *This Is Birmingham: The Story of the Founding and Growth of an American City.* Birmingham, AL: Southern University Press, 1969.

Historical and Statistical Review and Mailing and Shipping Guide of North Alabama (Illustrated) Embracing the Cities of Birmingham, Anniston, Gadsden, Huntsville, Decatur, Tuscaloosa and Bessemer, with Their Manufacturing and Mercantile Industries…and Sketches of Public and Private Citizens. Birmingham, AL: Southern Commercial Publishing Company, 1888.

Hollis, Tim. *Birmingham Broadcasting.* Charleston, SC: Arcadia Publishing, 2006.

———. *Birmingham's Theater and Retail District.* Charleston, SC: Arcadia Publishing, 2005.

———. *Pizitz: Your Store.* Charleston, SC: The History Press, 2010.

———. *Vintage Birmingham Signs.* Charleston, SC: Arcadia Publishing, 2008.

Hussey, A.R. *The Sign Painter: A Complete System and Set of Lessons for Beginners.* Chicago, IL: Pullman School of Lettering, 1916.

Jefferson County Heritage Book Committee. *The Heritage of Jefferson County, Alabama.* Clanton, AL: Heritage Publishing Consultants, 2002.

Jefferson County Historical Commission. *Birmingham and Jefferson County, Alabama.* Charleston, SC: Arcadia Publishing, 1998.

Johnson, Allen, Jr. *A Box of Trinkets.* Nashville, TN: Premium Press America, 2002.

Kelly, A. Ashmun. *The Expert Sign Painter.* West Chester, PA: Horace F. Temple Printing and Stationery Company, 1911.

Kennedy, Rick, and Randy McNutt. *Little Labels—Big Sound: Small Record Companies and the Rise of American Music.* Bloomington: Indiana University Press, 1999.

Kennedy, Rick, and Richard Lee Kennedy. *Jelly Roll, Bix, and Hoagy: Gennett Studios and the Birth of Recorded Jazz.* Bloomington: Indiana University Press, 1994.

Kern-Foxworth, Marilyn. *Aunt Jemima, Uncle Ben, and Rastus: Blacks in Advertising, Yesterday, Today, and Tomorrow.* Westport, CT: Greenwood Press, 1994.

Lewis, Pierce, and Marjorie Longenecker White. *Birmingham View: Through the Years in Photographs.* Birmingham, AL: Birmingham Historical Society, 1996.

Matthews, E.C. *How to Paint Signs and Sho'Cards.* New York: J.S. Ogilvie Publishing Company, 1920.

McMillan, Malcolm C. *Yesterday's Birmingham: Seeman's Historic Cities Series No. 18.* Miami, FL: Seeman Publishing, 1975.

Montage/Technala Yearbook. "Tyler Grocery Company Advertisement." Montevallo, AL: University of Montevallo, 1924.

———. "Young & Vann Supply Company Advertisement." Montevallo, AL: University of Montevallo, 1910.

New Orleans city directories. Various publishers, 1875–1900.

The New Patrida: The Story of Birmingham's Greeks. Birmingham, AL: Birmingfind, 1981.

Norell, Jeff. *The Italians: From Bisacquino to Birmingham.* Birmingham, AL: Birmingfind, 1981.

Pendergrast, Mark. *For God, Country and Coca-Cola: The Unauthorized History of the Great American Soft Drink and the Company That Makes It.* New York: Charles Scribner's Sons, 1993.

Pioneers of Greater Birmingham. Birmingham, AL: Jefferson County Historical Commission in cooperation with the Birmingham Area Chamber of Commerce, 1979.

Presbrey, Frank. *The History and Development of Advertising.* Garden City, NY: Doubleday, Doran & Company, 1929.

Rorer, Sarah Tyson Heston. *Snowdrift Secrets: Some Recipes for the Use of Snowdrift, the Perfect Shortening for All Cooking.* New York: Southern Cotton Oil Company, 1913.

Sanderson, Thomas W. *20th Century History of Youngstown and Mahoning County, Ohio, and Representative Citizens.* Chicago, IL: Biographical Publishing Company, 1907.

Satterfield, Carolyn Green. *Historic Sites of Jefferson County.* Revised ed. Birmingham, AL: Lowry Printing, 1985.

Schneider, David B., for the City of Birmingham, in collaboration with Main Street Birmingham, Inc. *An Architectural Guide to Downtown Ensley.* Birmingham, Alabama, 2009.

———. *Downtown Ensley & Tuxedo Junction: An Introductory History.* Birmingham, Alabama, 2009.

Sketches of Citizens of Birmingham. Indianapolis, IN: Citizens Historical Association, 1936–44. Bound into one volume by Birmingham Public Library, 1965.

Sloan, Earl S. *Sloan's Cook Book and Advice to Housekeepers.* Boston, MA: Dr. Earl S. Sloan, 1905.

Smith, Dennis. *Birmingham Bottlers 1883–1983.* Birmingham, AL: self-published, 2005.

———. *Kola Wars: Birmingham.* Birmingham, AL: self-published, 2007.

Southern Accent Yearbook. "Louis Saks Advertisement." Birmingham, AL: Birmingham-Southern College, 1907.

———. "Lucky Strike Advertisement." Birmingham, AL: Birmingham-Southern College, 1944.

———. "Tyler Grocery Company Advertisement." Birmingham, AL: Birmingham-Southern College, 1929.

———. "Young & Vann Supply Company Advertisement." Birmingham, AL: Birmingham–Southern College, 1923.

Southside-Highlands Report: Architectural & Historical Resources Preservation Recommendations. Birmingham, AL: Birmingham Historical Society, 1981.

Stage, [William]. *Ghost Signs: Brick Wall Signs in America.* Cincinnati, OH: ST Publications Inc., 1989.

Starr, Tama, and Edward Hayman. *Signs and Wonders: The Spectacular Marketing of America.* New York: Currency/Doubleday, 1998.

Thomas, Adam. *Apparitions of the Past: The Ghost Signs of Fort Collins.* Estes Park, CO: Historitecture, 2007.

Utz, Karen R., on behalf of the Sloss Furnaces Foundation. *Sloss Furnaces.* Charleston, SC: Arcadia Publishing, 2009.

Waldo, J. Curtis. *Visitor's Guide to New Orleans.* "E.F. Denechaud Advertisement." New Orleans, LA: Southern Publishing & Advertising House, 1875.

White, Marjorie Longenecker. *The Birmingham District: An Industrial History and Guide.* Birmingham, AL: Birmingham Historical Society, 1981.

———. *Downtown Birmingham: Architectural and Historical Walking Tour Guide.* Birmingham, AL: Birmingham Historical Society, 1977.

Wolburg, Joyce M. *Double Cola: The Story of the Underdog in the Soft Drink Industry.* Knoxville: University of Tennessee, 1993.

Wood, James Playsted. *The Story of Advertising.* New York: Ronald Press Company, 1958.

ESSAYS

Hulen, Tara, and Thomas Spencer. "In the 'Ham, the Hot Dog Rules." In *Cornbread Nation 1: The Best of Southern Food Writing.* Edited by John Egerton. Oxford: Center for the Study of Southern Culture, University of Mississippi, 2002.

Long, Laurie K. "A City with a Face: Street Art in Birmingham." In *Birmingham Then and Now: A Collection of Essays.* Edited by Ada Long. Birmingham: University of Alabama at Birmingham Honors Program, 1986.

McCarl, Patricia L. "Whiskey and Wild Women: Vice in the Early Days of Birmingham." In *Birmingham Then and Now: A Collection of Essays.* Edited by Ada Long. Birmingham: University of Alabama at Birmingham Honors Program, 1986.

MAGAZINE AND NEWSPAPER ARTICLES

Altoona Mirror. "Invents New Machine." November 13, 1917.

Archibald, John. "Morris Avenue Reborn: The One-Time Entertainment District Is Again Teeming with Activity, Now as Offices and Residential Lofts." *Birmingham News*, September 28, 1997.

Atlanta Constitution. "Burned Out Second Time." October 4, 1905.

Augusta Chronicle. "Signs of the Past." October 13, 2002.

Barber, Dean. "Auction Brings No Buyer for Decaying Hotel." *Birmingham News*, September 18, 1987.

Bell, Elma. "Red-Light Re-do: Former Area of Brothels Site of City's Next Big Historic Renovation." *Birmingham News*, August 25, 1999.

Benjamin, Patricia J. "Rub It On, Rub It In: A Brief History of Oils and Liniments Used in Massage." *Massage Therapy Journal* (Summer 2003).

Birmingham Age-Herald. "Hotel Opens on September 7." August 19, 1929.

Birmingham Historical Society Newsletter. "Motorcycle Mania" (February 2002).

Birmingham History Center Newsletter 1, no. 2. "On Exhibit—Motlow Brothers Distillers Letter" (March 1, 2011).

Birmingham News. "Berthon, Pauline Edith." June 27, 2010.

———. "Booth Funeral Held." November 23, 1931.

———. "Business Briefly: Turner Supply Buys Assets." June 15, 2000.

———. "Caiola, Joseph L." October 24, 2007.

———. "City's Brewing Industry Goes Back to 1884." July 13, 2000.

———. "Cosby Hodges." September 8, 1996.

———. "Grandeur Settles into Dust of Fate, Progress." December 19, 1971.

———. "Louis Saks, Pioneer Merchant, Succumbs at Residence in City." December 23, 1942.

———. "New Businesses." October 22, 1996.

———. "Remodeling Work Begun on Kessler's Downtown." July 1959. As quoted in *Birmingham Rewound.*

———. "Room Redo." December 8, 2007.

Birmingham Post. "Bells Herald Daughter's Return From New Hotel." September 18, 1929.

———. "Birmingham's New Hotel Among Finest in Nation." August 23, 1929.

———. March 2, 1923, front section.

Black, Tommy. "Cahaba Houses a 'Vanishing Breed.'" *Birmingham News*, July 19, 1981.

Bolton, Clyde. "In the Days of Moonshine and Revenuers…Stock Car Racing's Roots Go Back to Hauling Whiskey and Running from the Law." *Birmingham News*, April 19, 1998.

———. "Jokester Mechanic, Grayson Rose, to Be Inducted in Racing Hall of Fame." *Birmingham News*, December 6, 1998.

———. "State's Racing Pioneers Honored." *Birmingham News*, December 11, 1998.

Bolton, Mike. "Cancer Has Weakened Hodges, but Not His Love for Hunting." *Birmingham News*, May 5, 1996.

———. "It's Not Racing Without Cheatin'." *Birmingham News*, February 16, 2006.

Bowers, Paige. "Clark Byers, 89, Painter of Ads on Barn Roofs Across the East." *New York Times*, February 21, 2004.

Brown, Don. "City Under One Roof Opens Tomorrow." *Birmingham News*, August 24, 1960.

Bryant, Joseph D. "Glory Days Long Gone for Thomas Jefferson Hotel." *Birmingham Business Journal*, July 7, 2002.

Buchanan, Charles. "Ghost Tour." *Birmingham Magazine*, November 2010.

Carlton, Bob. "Bright Star's Jimmy and Nicky Koikos Go to New York to Receive James Beard Honor." *Birmingham News*, May 2, 2010.

———. "Drawing a Cold One: City Welcomes First Brew Pub." *Birmingham News*, March 9, 1995.

———. "Year of Alabama Food: Bright Star, Bessemer." *Birmingham News*, March 9, 2012.

Cranford Citizen. "Sloan's Liniment Advertisement." February 10, 1910.

Debro, Anita. "Vintage Sign in Downtown Bessemer Gets Restored by Neely Brothers." *Birmingham News*, August 3, 2011.

Diel, Stan. "Downtown B'ham Lucky Strike Bowling Alleys Sign Discovered." *Birmingham News*, February 24, 2011.

———. "Downtown Birmingham's Leer Tower Drawing Interest." *Birmingham News*, July 14, 2011.

———. "Signs of Our Past: Fading Advertising Still Decorates Downtown Buildings, but for How Long?" *Birmingham News*, December 31, 2006.

Dobrinksi, Rebecca. "Investing in the Past." *Magic City Post*, July 10, 2011. MagicCityPost.com.

Edge, John T. "Dog Day Afternoon: A Food Odyssey." *Birmingham News*, September 21, 2001.

Florence Times-Daily. "Hair Styling Contest Won by Ray Reed." February 16, 1948.

———. "Negley Beauty Shop Advertisement." October 19, 1952.

———. "Tip-Top Flour Advertisement." July 21, 1934.

Gadsden Times. "Company Purchasing Barber Dairies." September 13, 1998.

Gaskin, Tom. "Lyric's 'Birmingham Hot Dog' Sets Your Tongue Wagging." *Birmingham News*, May 30, 1996.

Godwin, Brent. *"Q&A: Claude B. Nielsen, Coca-Cola Bottling United Inc."* *Birmingham Business Journal*, June 24, 2011.

Hulen, Tara. "Getting Down to Business: Edgewood, Heart of Homewood, Boasts Strong Commercial Pulse." *Birmingham News*, March 9, 1994.

Irvin, David. "Whitfield Foods Turns 100 This Year." *Montgomery Advertiser*, March 2, 2006.

Lovelace, Craig. "Shaping Columbus: Joseph A. Jeffrey, Columbus' Coal-Mining King." *Columbus Business First*, February 24, 2012.

Maryland Insurance Administration. "Market Conduct Examination Report of the Life and Health Business of American-Amicable Life Insurance Company of Texas." January 25, 2002.

Metro Magazine. "Lyric Theatre Had Checkered Past." November, 8, 1978.

Morris, Philip. "Design Review at Work." *Design Alabama* 21 (2001).

Motor Age 7, no. 6. "Placed Buick Agencies" (February 9, 1905).

New York Times. "Light of Day and New Paint Refresh First Coca-Cola Sign." June 4, 1989.

Nicholson, Gilbert. "McBride Sign Closes, Owner Takes New Tack." *Birmingham Business Journal*, January 12, 2003.

———. "Young & Vann Building Gets $3.56M Overhaul." *Birmingham Business Journal*, March 7, 2004.

Paint, Oil, and Drug Review 51, no. 5. "Trade Items." (February 1, 1911).

Pierce, Phil. "Columbiana Crossing Business Owners Optimistic Despite Two Major Closings." *Birmingham News*, June 19, 1995.

Pittsburgh Press. "Republic Tires Advertisement." May 13, 1917.

Powelson, Richard. "First Color Television Sets Were Sold 50 Years Ago." *Pittsburgh Post-Gazette*, December 31, 2003.

Pratt, Ted. "Historic German Auto Building on the Market for $1.7 Million." *Birmingham News*, August 23, 2001.

———. "Jefferson Home Furniture to Close After 65 Years." *Birmingham News*, July 18, 1997.

———. "100 Years as a Family Business: Some Companies Have Found Successful Recipes for Longevity." *Birmingham News*, March 9, 1997.

———. "Yeilding to Shut Stores After 120 Years in City." *Birmingham News*, October 6, 1996.

Ratliff, Phillip. "Beyond Barbecue and Baklava: How Greek Immigrants Defined Birmingham." *Weld*, April 5, 2012.

Reading Eagle. "Tuxedo Tobacco Advertisement." January 20, 1913.

Robinson, Carol. "The Back-Tax Top 10: Drive to Collect Starts Paying Off." *Birmingham News*, March 30, 1995.

———. "Beloved Hot Dog Man Gus Dies at 81." *Birmingham News*, April 6, 2011.

Schaeffer, Randy S., and William E. Bateman. "Coca-Cola Painted Wall Signs." *Coca-Cola Collector's News*, February 1988.

Spencer, Thomas. "Living History Museum Sticks to Age-Old Art." *Birmingham News*, November 9, 2007.

———. "Long-Time Businesses Reflect City's Rich History: Travel Agency, Realty Company Pass Century Mark." *Birmingham News*, December 26, 2010.

State of Rhode Island Department of Business Regulation, Insurance Division. "Report on the Examination of Stonewall Insurance Company as of December 31, 2008." 2009.

Testa, Karen. "Fashionably Big: Missouri Company Grows from Overalls to Fashion Runways." *Ocala Star-Banner*, May 21, 1996.

Toledo Blade. "Refrigerated Biscuits Part of Food History." November 10, 2008.

Tomberlin, Michael. "Auctioneer for Stonewall Building Says Site Fit for Loft Development." *Birmingham News*, December 2, 1998.

———. "Building Future on City's Past: ONB, Leaders Seek to Reclaim 'Most Wanted' City Landmarks." *Birmingham News*, May 23, 2004.

———. "Center of Change: Old Young & Vann Building Becomes New Center for Regional Planning and Design." *Birmingham News*, August 24, 2003.

———. "City Condo-Mania: Phoenix Team Looks Next Door for Jefferson Lofts." *Birmingham News*, June 5, 2005.

———. "Downtown Dreams—Most Still Wanted: Renovation Slow for Prominent Buildings." *Birmingham News*, February 13, 2011.

———. "Downtown Dreams: Renovation Slow for Prominent Buildings." *Birmingham News*, February 13, 2011.

———. "Downtown Stonewall Project Hits Economic Roadblock." *Birmingham News*, August 19, 2008.

———. "Former Cabana Going Condo." *Birmingham News*, June 19, 2005.

———. "Influence of Birmingham Design Review Committee Widely Seen in Development." *Birmingham News*, April 4, 2012.

———. "Near Pizitz, New Plans Take Shape: Owners Look to Improve, Revamp Neighbor Sites." *Birmingham News*, September 24, 2010.

———. "New Breed of Redevelopers: Siblings Are Part of the Next Generation Helping to Reinvent Downtown." *Birmingham News*, January 10, 1999.

———. "Old Hotel Crumbles as Project Collapses." *Birmingham News*, May 5, 2009.

———. "Pizitz Building Draws Interest of Retailers." *Birmingham News*, April 23, 2010.

———. "Renovation Reveals Old Murals in Downtown Birmingham Building." *Birmingham News*, June 9, 2010.

———. "Screening Room, Neighboring Sites Set for Redevelopment." *Birmingham News*, October 17, 2008.

———. "Walgreens Told to Try Again; Lyric Sign Ok'd." *Birmingham News*, April 29, 2010.

Trombly, Richard. "Super-Regional Distribution." *Industrial Distribution*, May 2001.

Tuscaloosa News. "Morgenthau's Cleaners Advertisement." March 27 1949.

———. "Pizitz Beauty Salon Advertisement." September 18, 1949.

Victory, Dennis. "Days at the Races: Ex-News Sportswriter's Latests Book Calls on His Nascar Experience." *Birmingham News*, April 1, 2003.

Walsh, Maggie Hall. "History Blocking Adult Bookstore." *Birmingham News*, February 24, 1998.

Wheeler, Willard J. "In Birmingham, Alabama." *Printers' Ink* 29, no. 1 (July 5, 1899).

Williams, Roy L. "Bankruptcy Dims Glitter in Golbro: Once-Thriving Jewelry Store Chain Trims Operations to Ensure Survival." *Birmingham News*, August 28, 1994.

———. "Bankrupt Golbro to Close: 100-Year-Old Jewelry Chain Will Liquidate." *Birmingham News*, April 12, 1995.

———. "Birmingham Building's 1950s Advertising Mural Will Remain Visible." *Birmingham News*, April 28, 2012.

———. "Birmingham Design Review Committee Approves Plan to Paint Over Southside Mural." *Birmingham News*, April 25, 2012.

———. "Developer Considers Renewal Plan Beyond Birmingham's A.G. Gaston Motel Site." *Birmingham News*, February 21, 2008.

———. "Homegrown: Birmingham's Dixie Store Fixtures Celebrates Its 90th Anniversary This Year." *Birmingham News*, July 9, 2011.

———. "Hunter Furniture Closing After 89 Years as Mainstay." *Birmingham News*, October 15, 2009.

———. "Jefferson Home Sold to Leath." *Birmingham News*, May 13, 1994.

———. "Old Golbro Dies, New Golbro Emerges: Business Went into Bankruptcy, Reopened as Golbro Jewelry Center." *Birmingham News*, January 14, 1996.

WEBSITES AND BLOGS

American Masters. "Vaudeville," October 8, 1999. http://www.pbs.org/wnet/americanmasters/episodes/vaudeville/about-vaudeville/721.

Auer, Michael J. "Preservation Brief 25: The Preservation of Historic Signs." Technical Preservation Services, National Park Service, October 1991. http://www.nps.gov/hps/tps/briefs/brief25.htm.

Birmingham Public Library. "Alabama Inventors Database." http://bpldb.bplonline.org/db/inventors.

Buffalo Trace–Kentucky Straight Bourbon. "Albert Bacon Blanton." https://www.buffalotracedistillery.com/main.asp?page=history_blanton.

Carmichael, Mary. "Durham, N.C. Is Smokin'—No Bull!" Mental Floss, September 28, 2006. http://www.mentalfloss.com/blogs/archives/1978#ixzz262XQtiN8.

Centers for Disease Control and Prevention, Division of Nutrition, Physical Activity, and Obesity. "Healthier Food Retail: Beginning the Assessment Process in Your State or Community." http://www.cdc.gov/obesity/childhood/solutions.html.

City of Birmingham. "The City of Birmingham Zoning Ordinance," 2007. http://www.birminghamal.gov/pdf/pep/ZONING%20ORD.UPDATED2-8-2012.pdf.

Crush Soda Official Site. "All About Crush." http://www.crushsoda.com.

Double Cola Company. "Double Cola," 2012. http://www.double-cola.com/product/double-cola.

———. "The Story of the Double Cola Company." http://www.double-cola.com/history.

Erdreich, Jeremy. "…And Flickering Back On?" Bhamarchitect's Blog, April 27, 2012. http://constructbirmingham.wordpress.com/2012/04/27/and-flickering-back-on.

———. "Flickering Out." Bhamarchitect's Blog, April 25, 2012. http://constructbirmingham.wordpress.com/2012/04/25/flickering-out.

Find a Grave. "Samuel Thruston Ballard." http://www.findagrave.com/cgi-bin/fg.cgi?page=gr&GRid=28777914.

H.G. Hill Food Stores. "History." http://hghills.com/history.

Hollis, Tim. "Showplaces of the South." Birmingham Rewound. http://www.birminghamrewound. com/features/bham_theaters.htm.

Hormel Foods. "Celebrating 121 Years—Planning Ahead." http://www.hormelfoods.com/about/ history/default.aspx.

Joseph, Elliott. "Fading Fast." *Preservation*. National Trust for Historic Preservation, April 20, 2007. http://www.preservationnation.org/magazine/story-of-the-week/2007/fading-fast.html.

Kennedy, Robert C. "On This Day: Defacing the Beauties of Nature." *New York Times*, 2001. http:// www.nytimes.com/learning/general/onthisday/harp/1028.html.

The Lyric Theatre. "Theatre History." http://savethelyric.com/theatre-history.

Mooney, Phil. "Painted Wall Signs." Coca-Cola Conversations Blog. http://www.coca-colaconversations.com/2009/08/painted-wall-signs.html.

Morse, John. "Hot Dog Time Machine." *The Terminal*, April 12, 2010. http://bhamterminal.com/ mybirmingham/2010/04/12/hot-dog-time-machine.

———. "Meet Me in the Land of Grapico." 1731 Blog Avenue, April 18, 2011. http:// birminghamhistorycenter.wordpress.com/2011/04/18/meet-me-in-the-land-of-grapico.

Pepper Place. "History of Pepper Place." http://www.pepperplace.net/History_of_Pepper_ Place.html.

Preservation Durham. "Durham Tobacco Timeline." http://mainstreet.lib.unc.edu/projects/tobacco_ durham/index.php/documents/view/61.

Richardson, Lynn. "The Bull City—A Short History of Durham, North Carolina." Adapted from *Durham County: A History of Durham County, North Carolina*, by Jean Anderson. http://www. museumofdurhamhistory.org.

Royal Crown Cola International. "About Royal Crown: History." http://www.rccolainternational. com/about_royal_crown_history.aspx.

Southern Foodways Alliance. "Hot Dog-opolis," 2009. See on vimeo.com. http://www.vimeo. com/3460153.

Starr-Gennett Foundation. "J.T. Allison's Sacred Harp Singers." http://starrgennett.org/stories/ profiles/Allison%27s.htm.

———. "Overview of the History of the Starr Piano Company." http://starrgennett.org/stories/ history/index.htm.

Tennessee History for Kids. "Good to the Last Drop…Or Was It?" Adapted from *Fortunes, Fiddles and Fried Chicken: A Business History of Nashville*, by Bill Carey. http://www.tnhistoryforkids.org/ stories/maxwell_house.

United States Statutes at Large. Pure Food and Drug Act (1906). 59th Cong., Sess. I, Chp. 3915, 768–72. Cited as 34 U.S. Stats, 768. http://www.ncbi.nlm.nih.gov/books/NBK22116.

Vintage Ad Browser. "Sentinel Televisions Advertisement, 1952." http://www.vintageadbrowser. com/search?q=sentinel+television.

Wheelock. "History & Photos." http://www.wheelockhvac.com//green/History.html.

Which Came First on First Blog. "At First: How I Came to Be 'on First!'" January 5, 2011. http://whichcamefirstonfirst.com.

Zoominfo. "Berthon's Cleaners History." http://www.zoominfo.com/#!search/profile/person?personId=418945707&targetid=profile.

OTHER SOURCES

Birmingham, Alabama. Map, 1885. Norris, Wellge and Company, Milwaukee, Wisconsin. http://alabamamaps.ua.edu/historicalmaps/counties/jefferson/jefferson.html.

Birmingham, Alabama. Sanborn Fire Insurance Maps, 1888–1951. Sanborn Map Company, Pelham, New York. http://sanborn.umi.com.

Gennett Rarities: Recorded in Birmingham, Alabama & Richmond, Indiana 1927–1929. Sound recording. Toronto, ON: Jazz Oracle Phonograph Record Company, 1998. http://www.amazon.com/Gennett-Rarities-Recorded-Birmingham-1927-1929/dp/B000009PUP.

Nirenstein, Nathan. *Downtown Birmingham, Alabama.* Map, 1937. Nathan Nirenstein, Birmingham, Alabama. http://alabamamaps.ua.edu/historicalmaps/counties/jefferson/jeffersonb.html.

Reid, Ivan, and Peter De Rose. "Meet Me in the Land of Grapico." Sheet music. New Orleans, LA: J. Grossman's Sons, 1916.

About the Author

Charles Buchanan began noticing advertising at an early age. In fact, he proved to his parents that he could read by reciting the text on billboards during family road trips. Eventually, he would help to craft those words as an advertising copywriter, creating print ads and TV and radio commercials along with outdoor boards. An Alabama native, Charles is now a magazine editor at a university in Birmingham, where he continues to appreciate a punchy headline. He is also an artist who creates block prints inspired by the architecture, iconography and natural beauty of Birmingham. These have been featured on HGTV and on Alabama's tourism website, and their layered look takes a lot of inspiration from the city's fading ads.

Visit us at
www.historypress.net